What is Philosophy of Mind?

What is Philosophy of Mind?

Tom McClelland

polity

First published in 2021 by Polity Press

Polity Press
65 Bridge Street
Cambridge CB2 1UR, UK

Polity Press
101 Station Landing
Suite 300
Medford, MA 02155, USA

ISBN-13: 978-1-5095-3876-8
ISBN-13: 978-1-5095-3877-5(pb)

A catalogue record for this book is available from the British Library.

Library of Congress Cataloging-in-Publication Data

Names: McClelland, Tom, author.
Title: What is philosophy of mind? / Tom McClelland.
Description: Cambridge, UK ; Medford, MA, USA : Polity Press, 2021. | Series: What is philosophy? | Includes bibliographical references and index. | Summary: "The most student-friendly short introduction to philosophy of mind available"-- Provided by publisher.
Identifiers: LCCN 2020047693 (print) | LCCN 2020047694 (ebook) | ISBN 9781509538768 | ISBN 9781509538775 (pb) | ISBN 9781509538782 (epub)
Subjects: LCSH: Philosophy of mind.
Classification: LCC BD418.3 .M3625 2021 (print) | LCC BD418.3 (ebook) | DDC 128/.2--dc23
LC record available at https://lccn.loc.gov/2020047693
LC ebook record available at https://lccn.loc.gov/2020047694

Typeset in 11 on 13 pt Sabon by
Servis Filmsetting Ltd, Stockport, Cheshire
Printed and bound in Great Britain by Short Run Press

For further information on Polity, visit our website: politybooks.com

Contents

Acknowledgements

Many thanks to Pascal Porcheron at Polity Press for his invaluable guidance and to two anonymous referees for their insightful suggestions. Thanks, too, to all my students, past and present, for teaching me how to think about the philosophy of mind. I'd also like to thank Laura, Albus and Atticus for all their support. This book could not have been completed without the help of Yorkshire Tea.

1

The Mind and Its Problems

1.1 Philosophizing about the Mental

So what is philosophy of mind? Well, we all know what a mind is. Everyone has one, after all, and nothing could be more familiar to us than the contents of our own mind. Putting into words exactly what it means to have a mind can be very tricky, as can describing the different kinds of thing that happen in the mind. But we at least have some intuitive grip on the mind and on a whole host of familiar mental phenomena like perceptions, pains, beliefs, desires, emotions and intentions. We also know what philosophy is. Philosophy is the discipline that asks the big questions about life, the universe and everything. It asks metaphysical questions about the nature of reality, epistemological questions about our knowledge of reality, and normative questions about the value of things in reality. It grapples with these questions by challenging our most basic assumptions, analysing our most foundational concepts and constructing a clear and coherent framework for thinking about the world.

Putting this together, we can describe philosophy of

mind as a sub-discipline that investigates the mind philosophically. It asks metaphysical questions about what the mind is, about which things have minds and about how the mind fits into reality. It asks epistemological questions about how we know what's going on in our own minds and how we know about other minds. It even asks some normative questions about the value of having a mind and about how things with minds ought to be treated. And philosophy of mind deals with these questions by challenging our everyday assumptions about mental phenomena, probing the concepts we use to describe those phenomena and developing a better framework for thinking about the mind and its place in nature.

Philosophy is not, of course, the only discipline that has the mind as its target. The *cognitive sciences* are an interconnected family of disciplines that investigate the mind and mental phenomena. Cognitive science encompasses neuroscience, psychology, linguistics, artificial intelligence (AI) and aspects of anthropology. Given how successful these disciplines have been at providing insights into the mind, one might wonder what philosophy has to offer. Why not just hand over the big questions to cognitive scientists and give philosophers the day off? The answer is that these disciplines aren't in a position to deal with the kinds of question raised by the philosophy of mind.

Any scientific investigation of the mind will be built upon metaphysical assumptions: assumptions about what the mind is, about how the mind relates to the brain, and about the nature of specific mental phenomena like pain or love. But these are exactly the kinds of assumption that philosophy seeks to critique. Cognitive science also makes epistemological assumptions about the methods we should use to learn about mental phenomena. But these are again precisely the assumptions that philosophers call into question. One objective of philosophy of mind is to determine whether the cognitive sciences are well founded, and this isn't an objective that can be accomplished by the cognitive sciences themselves. Trying to use cognitive science to justify its own assumptions is like trying to jump on your own shadow – it's ill-conceived and ultimately futile. Of course, philosophers too will often have to make assumptions, but the difference is that none of these assumptions are built into the fabric of the discipline. For philosophers, everything is up for debate.

Another reason that the cognitive sciences are unsuited to answering philosophical questions is that these questions are so general in scope. Philosophy explores the big picture of how all of our knowledge fits together – what we know from our everyday experiences, what we know from the natural sciences and what we know from the cognitive sciences. But sciences proceed by zooming in on specific regions of the big picture. Each science picks out a special domain, such as language or intelligence, and investigates that domain without worrying too much about how it relates to the rest of the picture. So philosophy of mind again aims to offer something that science cannot: an overall picture of the mind and its place in the world.

None of this is to say that one way of investigating the mind is *superior* to the other. Philosophy has one role to play and science another. Nor is it to say that philosophy and science must be kept apart. Philosophy can do conceptual work that helps science to succeed and science can yield empirical insights that help philosophers to answer their conceptual questions. Indeed, a driving message of this book is that the history of philosophy of mind is best understood as a centuries-long dialogue between philosophy and science. Exactly how this give-and-take should work is a matter of some debate, but what's clear is that philosophical questions about the mental are unavoidable and that philosophy has an indispensable role to play in the study of the mind.

1.2 A Whistle-Stop Tour of the Mind

Since we're going to be asking philosophical questions about the mind, it will help to have a clearer idea of our subject matter. The mind is, after all, a highly complex and multifaceted thing. To know your way around the mind, you need to have a grip on the full range of mental phenomena that make up our mental lives. Let's start by examining the different mental states that someone has at a specific time.

Our subject – let's call her Mindy – is the striker for her university football team (by which I mean 'soccer' team). It's the cup final and, in the last minutes of the game, her team has been awarded a penalty kick. If she scores the penalty, her team will surely win. As she strides up to the penalty spot, what's going through Mindy's mind? She can hear the crowd cheering, taste the sweat dripping into her mouth, and smell the cut grass. She can feel the mud on her knees and the pain in her muscles. She sees a whole visual scene before her: the ball on the penalty spot, the goalkeeper in the goal, the crowd watching behind. She feels a buzz of excitement mixed with a pang of dread. She thinks about where to aim her shot. She wants to score and believes that the best way to do this is to go the opposite way to the goalkeeper. She remembers that the last time the goalkeeper faced a penalty she dived to the right of the goal and Mindy infers that she'll dive the same way today. She decides to aim for the left and imagines kicking the ball hard into the bottom left corner. She runs up to the ball, kicks it and scores. She feels a huge rush of elation and runs to her teammates to celebrate.

In those few moments, Mindy has experienced a whole variety of mental phenomena. Let's start with what Mindy *perceives*. We perceive things through our senses – a set of systems that register information about our environment through our sense organs. Mindy *hears* the crowd, *smells* the grass, *tastes* the sweat, *feels* the mud and *sees* the scene before her. This covers the five main senses: hearing, smell, taste, touch and sight. Mindy will also have perceptual states generated by two other sensory systems: the vestibular system, which is responsible for our sense of balance, and the proprioceptive system, which is responsible for our sense of where our body is positioned. Another thing Mindy experiences is the pain in her muscles. This might be classified as a bodily sensation, like the feeling of mud on her knees. Alternatively, it might be classified as a kind of 'hedonic feeling'. On this view, feelings like pain or pleasure tell us how good or bad something is rather than conveying sensory information.

Now let's consider Mindy's *emotions*. She experiences excitement, dread and once she's scored the goal – elation. Each emotion has several different aspects. Mindy's feeling of elation, for example, has a *physiological* component: her heart rate and blood pressure go up. The emotion also constitutes a kind of *evaluation* of the situation Mindy is in: it presents the goal to Mindy as being a good thing in some way. The emotion manifests itself in Mindy's *behaviour*: she sprints to celebrate with her teammates. It also manifests itself in her *expressions*: her eyebrows raise, her mouth opens, her arms go up in the air. It's a matter of some debate where to locate the emotion itself in all this. Perhaps elation is something that causes these things to happen, or perhaps being elated is just an amalgam of all these things. It's also hard to pin down what the *experience* of an emotion contains: is the feeling of elation just the feeling of your heart rate increasing, your facial expression lifting and so on, or is there also some distinctive feeling of elation separate from these peripheral things?

Next up are Mindy's *thoughts*. Thoughts come in various forms, many of which Mindy exemplifies. Her thoughts include: a *desire* to score; a *belief* that scoring is best achieved by going the opposite way to the goalkeeper; a *memory* that the goalkeeper went right in the past; another *belief* that the goalkeeper will go right again; an *intention* to kick the ball to the left; and an *imaginative* experience of scoring the goal. The first thing to notice about these different thoughts is how they fit together. Her intention is justified by a rational process involving her beliefs, her desires and her memories. Reasoning is not a specific mental state but rather a mental *process* that unfolds over time and that encompasses all sorts of different mental states. How Mindy *reasons* about her situation plays a big role in determining what she thinks. This is quite different to perception – when Mindy looks at the goal she sees the goalkeeper, and no amount of reasoning can stop her from seeing the goalkeeper. It's also quite different to emotion – when Mindy feels an emotion, she can't easily reason herself into having a different emotion. We should stop short of claiming that perception and emotion are *completely* unresponsive to reasoning. Sometimes the way we perceive or feel about a situation is influenced by our rational thoughts. Nevertheless, there is a clear sense in which perceiving and feeling are outside our direct rational control in a way that thinking is not.

Another thing to notice about Mindy's thoughts is that they each share a common structure. Bertrand Russell (1872–1970) introduced the term *propositional attitude* to describe the different mental attitudes that we can take towards a given content. In the sentence 'Mindy believes that the goalkeeper will go left', the propositional attitude is *belief* and the proposition is *that the goalkeeper will go left*. Propositions are typically designated using a 'that' clause, and a propositional attitude is typically specified by whatever verb precedes the word 'that'. Propositions are things that can be true or false. The proposition that the goalkeeper will go left, for instance, is true if the goalkeeper in fact goes left and false if not.

Notice that Mindy can adopt different attitudes

towards the same proposition: she can *hope* the goal-keeper will go left, *desire* that the goalkeeper will go left, *imagine* that the goalkeeper will go left and so on. And she can also adopt the same attitude towards different propositions: she can believe that it's the cup final, believe that she's about to score, believe that tonight will be a riotous party and so on. All these different thoughts have the same structure: they are constituted by a propositional content and a mental attitude towards that content. This list makes the structure more explicit by italicizing the propositional attitude and underlining the proposition:

> Mindy *desires* that she will score the penalty
> Mindy *imagines* that she will score the penalty
> Mindy *remembers* that the goalkeeper went left in the past
> Mindy *intends* that she will kick the ball to the left-hand side of the goal
> Mindy *believes* that the goalkeeper will go left
> Mindy *believes* that scoring is best achieved by going the opposite way to the goalkeeper

Notice that the first two thoughts are constituted by Mindy having different propositional attitudes to the same proposition, and that the last two thoughts are constituted by Mindy having the same propositional attitude to different propositions. The concept of propositional attitudes offers a useful way of capturing how different thoughts resemble and differ from one another.

One complication here is that some of these thoughts involve *more* than just adopting a particular propositional attitude. For instance, when Mindy remembers that the goalkeeper went left in the past, she might have a vague mental image of their last dive. Similarly, when Mindy imagines scoring, she might have a vague mental image of the ball hitting the back of the net. Here it seems that Mindy's thoughts have a kind of *perception-like* component that would need to be included in a complete account of thought.

The final group of mental states we will consider are

volitions. We have seen lots of different mental states leading up to Mindy stepping forward and kicking the ball, but none of these mental states are enough to make Mindy actually *do* anything. Even once she's reasoned through what to do, even once she's formed an intention to go for the bottom-left corner, a volition is needed to put her body into motion. This volition might be described as an act of will. Volitions are the things that turn thought into action – they are the mental states that make things happen. Some hold that this concept of volitions overcomplicates matters. They argue that intentions can cause actions and that there's no need for a third kind of mental state mediating between the two. For our purposes, we can remain neutral on whether we really have volitions.

The states we've considered have all been *conscious* mental states – states of which Mindy is aware. But there are good reasons for thinking that our conscious mental life is just the tip of the iceberg, and that below the surface there are countless *un*conscious mental states. Some unconscious mental states can easily be brought into consciousness. You have the unconscious belief that Paris is the capital of France, but now that I've raised the topic of France's capital, that belief will have become conscious. Other unconscious mental states are much harder to retrieve. You might have an unconscious desire to murder your neighbour that only becomes conscious after months of psychotherapy. There might even be mental states that can *never* enter our consciousness. Your visual experience is the product of many stages of sensory processing and what goes on in the early stages of this process could well be inaccessible to us.

Many of the mental states we've considered come in conscious and unconscious varieties. The propositional attitudes offer some clear cases. Although Mindy is conscious of some of her beliefs, countless others of her beliefs are unconscious. She has beliefs about the history of the World Cup, beliefs about what's on her bookshelf at home, beliefs about the capitals of European countries, and so on. The same goes for desires. Mindy has a desire to get new football boots, a desire to learn to juggle and a desire to go travelling, but none of these desires are conscious while she's taking the penalty kick. Memories are another good case. Mindy has memories of her childhood, memories of last week's training session and memories of this morning's breakfast, but these memories are all unconscious. What about imagination? Can Mindy unconsciously imagine that she's going to be made captain? The answer's not so clear, but it's at least a live possibility that there are such unconscious imaginings.

Moving on to perception, psychological research has revealed that some perceptual states occur unconsciously. In subliminal perception, your mind registers a stimulus without you being aware of it. Let's say that the big screen at the football ground quickly flashes an advert for Jaffa Cakes. Mindy could perceive this advert, without even consciously experiencing it. Later on, she might even find herself with an inexplicable craving for Jaffa Cakes! The sensation of pain is an interesting case. It's tempting to say that you can't be in pain without that pain being conscious. But what if Mindy were to say, 'I didn't notice the pain in my ankle'? Should we conclude that Mindy had an unconscious pain or that the pain only started when Mindy started to have a conscious experience of pain? To answer this, we'd need to refine our understanding of what it is to be in pain and, indeed, our understanding of what it is for a mental state to be conscious.

Can you have emotions you aren't conscious of? We can imagine Mindy saying, 'It was only after the final whistle that I realized how nervous I'd been'. Perhaps this describes an unconscious emotion of nervousness. If you're angry at someone all day, must you be conscious of your anger all day or can your anger sometimes be bubbling away unconsciously? The answer will again depend on how we understand the nature of emotions and the nature of consciousness, but it's certainly an open possibility that our unconscious mind is populated by emotions.

What about volitions? On the one hand, you could argue that volitions have to be conscious. It's not clear how something could be an act of will if it's unconscious. On the other hand, there are lots of actions we perform without any conscious volition. When absent-mindedly driving a familiar road, for example, perhaps each change of gear is the result of an unconscious volition. Again, it's an open question.

1.3 The Mark of the Mental

The foregoing demonstrates the sheer diversity of what happens in the mind. Pains are as different to beliefs as beliefs are to perceptions. We bundle these diverse phenomena under the heading of 'mental', but what is it that makes a state mental? To say that Mindy has a certain 'state' is just to say that Mindy has some property at a particular time. And there are countless non-mental properties that Mindy has, such as having a body temperature of 37.1° Celsius. But why don't they qualify as mental?

Consider the table on the following page. This looks like an intuitive way of organizing Mindy's states. Although states like Mindy's muscle fatigue can *cause* mental states like the feeling of achy muscles, it remains clear that muscle fatigue itself is non-mental. So what determines whether a state goes in the first column or the second? We can ask the same question about the *processes* Mindy is undergoing. A process is a sequence of states that unfolds over time. For instance, Mindy is in the process of reasoning about where to aim her shot and in the process of digesting her lunch. But what makes the former process mental and the latter non-mental? To answer this, we need to find some defining

Table 1.1 Mental and Non-Mental Properties

MENTAL	NON-MENTAL
Perceiving the football	Having a temperature of 37.1° Celsius
Feeling an ache in her muscles	Having a heart rate of 125 beats per minute
Feeling excited	Having a blood pressure of 100/70
Believing that the goalkeeper will go left	Having muscle fatigue
Desiring that she will score	Being well hydrated
Remembering that the goalkeeper went left before	Being 6ft tall
Having an intention to kick the ball	Being in good physical health

feature of mentality   a feature possessed by everything in the mental column but nothing in the non-mental column. This elusive feature is known as *the mark of the mental*.

A tempting proposal is that mental states are distinguished by being states of the mind. Notice that everything in the first column is a state of Mindy's mind while everything in the second column is a state of Mindy's body. The problem with this proposal is that it just relocates the question we were trying to answer. Now we face the question of what makes something a state of the mind rather than a state of the body and we're no better off than we were. Another possible response is that there is no mark of the mental. We apply the label 'mental' to some states and not others, but our groupings are more or less arbitrary. On this view, there's no interesting feature that marks out all the states in the first column. One difficulty with this proposal is that grouping mental states together seems far from arbitrary. Intuitively, there is something these states have in common, even if that 'something' is hard to pin down. The sceptical response would also be bad news for our theorizing about the mind. We want to understand what mental states are, how we know about them and which things possess them. Anyone claiming that the category 'mental' is spurious will have to deny that these are worthwhile questions to investigate because they employ arbitrary categories.

A more promising proposal is that the mark of the mental is *intentionality*. The word 'intentionality' sounds like it should have something to do with a person's intentions, but this appearance is misleading. The word is derived from medieval Latin, and to have intentionality is to be *about* something. Mindy's perceptual experience, for example, is a perception *of* the football. So although her perceptual state is something in her mind, that state is *about* something beyond itself, namely the football. We can call the target of an intentional state *an intentional object*. Going through Mindy's other mental states, it's not too hard to pick out their intentional objects. Her achy feeling is *about* her muscles, her excitement is *about* her prospective goal, her desire is *about* scoring and her belief and memory are *about* the goalkeeper. In contrast, Mindy's non-mental states don't seem to be about anything. Mindy's height and muscle fatigue aren't about anything – they just exist without pointing beyond themselves.

An interesting feature of intentionality is that something can have an intentional object even when that object does not exist. A desire to find the Holy Grail is *about* the Holy Grail, even if no such object exists. A perceptual experience of a floating dagger is *about* a dagger, even though no such dagger is present. A belief in fairies is *about* fairies, even though there are no such creatures. We can make sense of this distinctive feature of intentionality by making an analogy with paintings. Some paintings are paintings of *real* things. Holbein's portrait of Henry VIII, for example, is of a real flesh-and-blood person. Other paintings are not of real things. Burne-Jones's painting *The Beguiling of Merlin* is a painting of Merlin, even though no such magician exists. So the fact that a painting is *about* something does not entail that thing exists. Similarly, a mental state being about something does not entail that thing is real. Mental states and paintings both point beyond themselves to something else, and they can do so regardless of whether there's anything real they are pointing to (this feature of intentionality is a philosophical rabbit hole down which we won't be going, but some readings that do venture down the hole can be found at the end of the chapter).

So far we've seen that at least some mental states have the property of intentionality and some non-mental states lack intentionality. But for intentionality to be the mark of the mental, something much stronger is needed: it must be the case that *all* and *only* mental phenomena have intentionality. The thesis that intentionality is necessary and sufficient for mentality was named *Brentano's thesis* after Franz Brentano (1838–1917). Although this idea has a long history running back at least to Aristotle, Brentano made a particularly influential case for it. One motivation for Brentano's thesis is the thought that to have a mind is to have a *perspective* on the world – a point of view. Mindy has one perspective on the world, the goalkeeper has a different perspective, and the referee another. The mindless football, on the other hand, has no perspective at all. Nor do the goalposts or the referee's whistle. Having a perspective means having a perspective *on* or *about* something. So perspectives come hand-in-hand with intentionality. Mindy's perspective on the world is made up of all her intentional states: her beliefs about things in the world, her perceptions of them, her feelings about them, and so on. The goalkeeper's perspective is made up of a completely different set of mental states: different beliefs, perceptions, feelings and so on. What makes those states mental states is that they are constituents of a perspective, and what makes them constituents of a perspective is their intentionality. Mindy's non-intentional states cannot be constituents of her perspective on the world, and this is what makes them non-mental. If you buy into this equation of minds with perspectives, you're a long way towards agreeing with Brentano's thesis.

To properly evaluate Brentano's thesis we need to consider whether it is vulnerable to counter-examples. Can we undermine Brentano's thesis with a non-mental case of intentionality? Well, we've seen already that paintings can have intentionality, like a portrait being *of* Henry VIII. Similarly, the map in my drawer is about Cambridge, the book on my desk is about philosophy and the reading on my thermostat is about the temperature. All of these things have intentional objects, yet none of them plausibly have mental states. Advocates of Brentano's thesis deal with such cases by arguing that these things only have intentionality *because we give it to them*. The painting is a painting of Henry VIII (rather than of his brother or of a fictional king) because that's who Holbein *meant* it to be of. The map is of Cambridge because the map-makers *designed* it to be. And the reading on the thermostat is about the temperature because that is the *function* it was given. A bunch of stuff happening in a box on the wall is *meaningless* without the wider context of people who design and use thermostats. On this view, one of the things that beings with *real* intentionality can do is imbue non-mental things with this kind of derivative intentionality. But non-derivative intentionality remains an exclusively mental property.

Can we undermine Brentano's thesis with a mental state that is non-intentional? It's unlikely that perception will provide such a counter-example. We normally describe our perceptual states in terms of what they're about – a perception *of* a cat, or *of* a cup or *of* a cake. In fact, it is hard to see how something could be a perception without being a perception *of* something. It's also unlikely that propositional attitudes will provide a counter-example. A propositional attitude is *about* whatever figures in the proposition. It also looks like intentions are inevitably intentional (though not because of the superficial similarity of the terms). Intentions are directed at whatever they are intentions *to do*. Pains might cause more trouble. One might argue that pains aren't really about anything – they just are. Emotions can also cause difficulties. Although emotions like Mindy's elation have a clear intentional object, other emotions seem to be undirected. Your mood might be cheerful, or grumpy, or melancholy, yet none of these emotions need to be about anything in particular. Maybe we can say that these emotions are *about the world in general* but there would have to be good arguments for understanding them that way.

The claim that intentionality is the mark of the mental certainly deserves to be taken seriously. But even if we stop short of advocating Brentano's thesis, the foregoing provides us with something useful. First, it gives us some idea of how to draw the line between the mental and the non-mental, and thus of how to delineate the subject matter of philosophy of mind. Second, it gives us the valuable concept of intentionality to put in our conceptual toolkit. My initial sketch of what was going on in Mindy's mind was a sketch of her perspective – her take on the world – with different mental states contributing to that perspective in their own distinctive ways. Understanding the mind will at least partly be a matter of understanding someone's perspective, and we can apply that insight as we begin to explore the big questions that define the philosophy of mind.

1.4 The Three Big Questions

The mind invites a huge range of philosophical questions. Some of these we've come across in the last two sections – questions about the nature of perception, emotion, pain and so on, questions about the mark of the mental, perspectives and intentionality. And there are countless other questions that we won't even touch upon. My focus in this book will be on the Three Big Questions:

1 **The Mind and Matter Question:** What is the relationship between mind and matter?
2 **The Knowledge Question:** How do we acquire knowledge of our own minds and the minds of others?
3 **The Distribution Question:** Which things have minds and what kind of mind do they have?

So what marks these out as the questions most deserving of our attention? Over the rest of this section, we'll see that how we answer has important ramifications for how we answer the smaller questions. It's hard to give an account of the nature of pain, for example, without taking a stance on the relationship between mind and matter. And over the rest of this book we'll see that the most important theories in philosophy of mind are defined by how they answer the Big Questions. In fact, the whole history of philosophy of mind can helpfully be framed as the history of thought on these questions. With that in mind, let's consider each question in turn.

1.4.1 *The Mind and Matter Question*

The Mind and Matter Question invites us to make sense of how the mind fits into the material world. The material world is the world of matter – of physical objects distributed in space and time and governed by the laws of physics. Material objects include everything from molehills to mountains to meteors. But all these different things are made out of the same kind of stuff, namely matter. If you want to know about matter, ask a physicist. They'll tell you that there's a small set of fundamental particle types – things like quarks and leptons – that make up the entire universe. And the behaviour of those particles is governed by a small set of physical laws. Think of it like a giant Lego set: from a few types of brick and some basic rules governing how they fit together, a near-infinite variety of things can be made. To be a material object is to be either one of the basic physical building blocks of the material world, or to be something made out of those basic physical building blocks. So our question is whether the mind is constituted by physical building blocks or whether it introduces a whole new immaterial constituent to reality.

Materialists (aka physicalists) claim that there are no immaterial entities: that everything in the universe is constituted by the great material Lego set. Minds are no exception to this. Mindy's mind is constituted by a material object – presumably her brain. The challenge for the materialist is to make sense of how this could be so. How can Mindy's beliefs be a state of Mindy's brain? How can her decisions be a neural process? How can her perceptions be a sparking of neurons? Dualists adopt the anti-materialist view that the world includes at least some immaterial entities, namely minds. Distinct from Mindy's physical body is a non-physical mind – something that cannot be constituted by the physical building blocks described by physics. The challenge for the dualist is to make sense of where immaterial minds come from and how they're connected to the brain.

A key battleground for materialists and dualists is *causation*. Mindy's visual experience is *caused* by physical events such as light hitting her retina in a particular way. And Mindy's intention to kick the ball *causes* the physical event of her kicking it. How can we make sense of these causal interactions? For materialists, these interactions take place *within* the material world. The story of Mindy's penalty kick is a completely physical story, and the challenge for materialists is to make sense of how Mindy's mental states fit within that story. For dualists, these interactions take place *between* physical and non-physical things. The story of Mindy's penalty kick involves both events in the material world and events in Mindy's immaterial mind, and the challenge for dualists is to make sense of how these two kinds of event hook up. The challenges here run deep, and both sides must confront the possibility that the apparent interactions between mind and body are not as they seem. Perhaps Mindy's perceptual experiences aren't really caused by her environment and perhaps her intentions aren't really the cause of her actions. This is a threat we'll be coming back to throughout the book.

How we answer the Mind and Matter Question can have huge implications for how we see ourselves and how we live our lives. Do we have a special place in nature, standing apart from the world of material entities, or is the mind smoothly continuous with the rest of the material world? Do we come into existence when our brain comes into existence or might our minds predate our bodies? Do we die when our body dies or could the mind survive our bodily death? Are we really responsible for our actions or is our behaviour outside our control? Each of these urgent questions comes back to the core question of how mind and matter are related.

1.4.2 *The Knowledge Question*

Metaphysics asks about the nature of reality and the Mind and Matter Question is a central question in the metaphysics of mind. The Knowledge Question, by contrast, is an epistemological question about our knowledge of mental states: how do I know what's going on in my own mind or in the minds of others? The first thing to notice is that the way you know about your own mind is quite different to the way you know about other minds. You can only know about Mindy's muscle pain from its outward signs – things like her facial expression or her verbal reports – but she knows about her muscle pain from the inside. There's thus an *epistemic asymmetry* between knowledge of one's own mind and knowledge of other minds.

It's tempting to say that we know our own minds via a kind of inner sense. Just as Mindy knows what's going on around her through perception, she knows what's going on in her own mind through *introspection*. But what is this introspection and how does it work? We can also ask about how *secure* our self-knowledge is. Can you think you are in a mental state but be wrong? Perhaps Mindy can misidentify her nervousness as excitement, but it's harder to make sense of her being wrong that she's in pain. Can you be in a mental state without knowing that you are? We can make sense of Mindy having memories she doesn't know about, but it's harder to make sense of her failing to know that she's in pain.

What about our knowledge of other minds? Our knowledge of other minds seems less secure. Mindy knows her own intentions quite clearly but has a much harder time working out which way the goalkeeper intends to dive. Does she learn about the goalkeeper's mind by perceiving her behaviour, by imagining her point of view, or by some combination of the two? If the goalkeeper acts like she wants to win the game, how does Mindy know she's not just *pretending* to have this desire? If the goalkeeper reports liking the smell of old socks, how does Mindy know that socks smell the same way to the goalkeeper as they do to her? Can we ever really *know* what's going on in the goalkeeper's mind or are we effectively just guessing? Could brain scans and advanced psychological investigation give us more direct access to the goalkeeper's mind, or are her mental states always hidden from us? How confident can we be that the goalkeeper even *has* a mind?

These epistemological questions are bound up with the metaphysical questions discussed earlier. If the mind is a material thing, then we need an account of how we know about our brain states and the brain states of others. If, on the other hand, the mind is immaterial, we need an account of how we can gain knowledge of these special non-physical states. These epistemological questions also have deep practical and ethical implications. When is it wrong to doubt someone's report of what's going on in their mind? Is it ever right to think that you know what someone wants better than they do? Can a juror ever really know that the accused intended to kill? Can a probation officer ever really know that a murderer doesn't desire to kill again? Our answers to these more concrete epistemological questions will be shaped by our answer to the Knowledge Question.

1.4.3 The Distribution Question

There are lots of things in the world, but which of them have minds? If you're watching the football game, you'll be pretty sure about the distribution of minds. You'll be confident that Mindy, the goalkeeper and the referee each has a mind. You'll also be confident that the ball, the goalposts and the referee's whistle don't have minds. But is this confidence well founded? And in many circumstances we're not so confident about the distribution of minds. Does a newborn baby have a mind? What about a foetus, or a zygote? Does your pet cat have a mind? What about a bat, a bee or an octopus? Should we attribute minds to trees, to plants or to viruses? Could there ever be an AI with its own mind? What about the internet, a smartphone or a self-driving car? Might it be that *everything* has a certain level of mindedness and that mentality pervades the universe? Or might it be that *nothing* does and that the whole idea of minds is a myth?

Once we've decided which things have minds, there remains the further question of what *kind* of mind they have. If a foetus has a mind, is it a *conscious* mind or a mind populated only by unconscious mental states? If an octopus has a mind, is it a *rational* mind like ours or a bundle of instinctive mental processes? If a self-driving car has a mind, is it an *emotional* mind with feelings of love and hate or is it emotionally inert? Besides asking these general questions about the distribution of consciousness, rationality and emotion, we can ask some more specific questions about the distribution of specific mental state types. For instance, which of these beings can feel pain and which cannot?

The Distribution Question has an epistemological aspect. How do we *know* whether something has a mind or what kind of mind it has? What criteria should we be applying and how confidently can we apply them? It also has a metaphysical aspect. What does it take for something to have a mind? What does it take for that mind to be rational, conscious or emotional? Does it involve something immaterial or is it a case of having the right physical properties? Could something without a biological brain have a mind? Could something without a physical body have a mind?

Our answer to the Distribution Question has enormous implications for how we interact with the people, creatures and artefacts around us. If we learn that the goalkeeper doesn't really have a mind, then how we treat her would immediately change. It would alter our expectations of her, the duties we feel towards her and the rights we attribute to her. Whether something has a mind can be a deciding factor in whether it deserves our moral consideration. The question of when a developing infant acquires a mind has great ethical import. Well into the 1970s, it was routine to give babies surgical procedures without anaesthetic. Why? Because the surgeons thought that babies hadn't yet developed minds capable of suffering so there was no need to risk giving them anaesthetic. It looks like the surgeons were making a huge ethical mistake here, and this mistake was built on their erroneous answer to the Distribution Question.

Something similar applies to our treatment of non-human organisms. You needn't feel guilty about standing on a daisy because you don't think that daisies have minds, but you ought to feel guilty about standing on a cat. So in order to treat organisms the right way, we really ought to know where in the tree of life minds start to emerge. AI stretches our moral imagination even further. You wouldn't feel guilty about sending a self-driving car to the scrap-heap, but is your indifference justified? One problem here is that we tend to be on the lookout for minds *like ours*. Could daisies or cars have minds that we fail to recognize because they're so totally unlike our own? And once we consider the possibility of completely different kinds of mind, the field of possible minds gets even broader. Maybe molecules have minds. Maybe planets do. Maybe the universe as a whole forms a vast '*über*-mind' of which we are all a part. If any of these possibilities are true, it could completely change how we act.

1.5 A Plan of Action

Over the next five chapters, we'll be looking at the key positions in philosophy of mind – the main 'theories of the mental'. These theories are defined by the answers they offer to the Three Big Questions, so by the time we're finished you'll have a decent grip on how to approach those questions. We'll be looking at the main theories of the mental in historical order, running from Descartes' work in the seventeenth century right up to contemporary debates in the field. One advantage of this is that it allows us to see how each new theory relies on its predecessors, building on their successes and attempting to overcome their failures. Another advantage is that it allows us to see how philosophy of mind interacts with the science of its time, drawing on scientific insights and challenging scientific assumptions. Furthermore, it allows us to see how philosophers living in different centuries can nevertheless be cut from the same cloth, adopting similar approaches to the puzzles of the mind. The following is an overview of our journey:

Chapter 2 explores Descartes' dualism. The seventeenth century saw great progress in our scientific understanding of the material world. Descartes, a scientist in his own right, asked how the mind would fit into this emerging picture. He argued that the mind must be an immaterial substance that stands apart from the material world but that is able to interact with it via the body. But Descartes' arguments faced a flurry of objections that still haunt dualists today.

Chapter 3 jumps ahead to the early to mid-twentieth century and introduces two materialist theories of mind. Behaviourism argues that mental states are nothing more than patterns of behaviour, and identity theory argues that mental states are nothing more than brain states. These theories were inspired by the emerging sciences of brain and behaviour and promised to overcome the failings of dualism. But each theory faced problems of its own.

Chapter 4 takes us to the mid- to late twentieth century and the computer revolution. According to functionalism, the mind is akin to a computer with our brain acting as the hardware on which the software of the mind runs. We look at how functionalism improved on other materialist theories to become the leading theory of the mental.

Chapter 5 looks at a problem for materialism that gained special traction at the end of the twentieth century – the Problem of Consciousness. A range of striking thought-experiments suggest that theories like functionalism cannot explain what our mental lives *feel* like on the inside. Conscious experience is thus an explanatory residue that requires special treatment. I look at two radical ways of dealing with this explanatory residue: a partial reversion to dualism on the one hand and a flat denial that conscious experience exists on the other.

Chapter 6 offers a brief overview of the contemporary scene in philosophy of mind. We will explore how recent work has enhanced our understanding of the Three Big Questions and how philosophy of mind has become integrated with the cognitive sciences. I'll also take a look at how philosophy of mind might develop in the future.

In one sense, the overview of philosophy of mind that I will offer won't be especially opinionated. I'll be presenting mainstream views and keeping some of my more eccentric opinions to myself. But in another sense the overview I offer will inevitably be opinionated. The philosophy of mind is a big field, so my selection of which ideas to discuss in this short book reflects my opinions on what's most important in the discipline. One way to get the benefit of some different perspectives is to engage with the suggested readings at the end of each chapter, which are arranged in recommended reading order.

Key Concepts

Anti-materialism: the view that materialism is false and at least some entities are non-physical.
Brentano's thesis: the thesis that intentionality is the mark of the mental, i.e. that all and only mental states have the property of being *about* things beyond themselves.
Epistemic asymmetry: the fact that we each know about our own mental states in a way that others cannot.
Intentionality: the property of being *about* something. The belief that tea is restorative is *about* tea and has tea as its 'intentional object'. Not all intentional objects actually exist.
Materialism: the view that everything, including

mental states, is ultimately constituted by physical entities.

Mark of the mental: a feature that all and only mental states have, differentiating the mental from the physical.

Propositional attitudes: a mental attitude taken towards a propositional content. If you believe that tea is restorative, the proposition is *that tea is restorative* and the attitude is *believing*.

References and Further Reading

- Tim Crane (2001), *Elements of Mind: An Introduction to the Philosophy of Mind*, Oxford: Oxford University Press. This excellent introduction explores how all the different kinds of mental state fit together. Crane's focus is on intentionality and the claim that intentionality is the mark of the mental.
- Franz Brentano (1911 [1874]), *Psychology from an Empirical Standpoint*, London: Routledge and Kegan Paul. Excerpt reprinted in David J. Chalmers (ed.) (2021), *Philosophy of Mind: Classical and Contemporary Readings*, 2nd edn, New York: Oxford University Press. This is the original formulation of the view that would later be known as Brentano's thesis.

2

Descartes' Dualism

2.1 The Mechanical Philosophy

René Descartes (1596–1650) was a key figure in the Scientific Revolution and lived through a period of immense intellectual change. The revolution had started, not long before Descartes' birth, with the publication of Copernicus's *On the Revolutions of the Heavenly Spheres* (1543). Within Descartes' lifetime, Galileo published his *Dialogue Concerning the Two Chief World Systems* (1632). And shortly after Descartes' death, Newton would publish his groundbreaking *Principia* (1687). Science was beginning to construct a rich and systematic account of the natural world – an account that Descartes himself helped to build. Descartes wrote extensively on the scientific method and his pioneering work in geometry would go on to shape Newton's physics.

According to the 'mechanical philosophy' that Descartes helped develop, the workings of the natural world are akin to the workings of a machine. Just as a clock is made of discrete parts, such as gears and springs, so too are material bodies constituted of smaller material parts. And just as the movements of a clock are explained by the movements of its parts, the movements of any material body arc explained by the movements of its constituents. For example, the clock striking twelve is explained by the movement of cogs that push the hour hand and trigger the chiming mechanism. Similarly, the movements of a cat are explained by the movements of its tendons and muscles. Crucially, the movements of a mechanism and its parts are wholly predictable. Given the state the clock was in a moment ago, it was inevitable that this would be its current state. And given the clock's current state, its next state is likewise inevitable. According to the mechanical philosophy, the movements of the natural world are similarly deterministic. Every movement of a material body is governed by the laws of nature – laws that apply in all places and at all times. The current state of the universe is thus the inevitable result of its preceding state, and the succeeding state of the universe will be the inevitable result of its current state. And this mechanistic framework applies at all scales, whether it be to the movements of a speck of dust, a human body or a distant planet.

This enticing picture of the natural world invites an obvious question: how does the mind fit in? This is the question that Descartes sought to answer. After all, the mind doesn't *seem* to be a machine made up from smaller parts, nor does it *seem* to follow a deterministic trajectory. And the great machine of the natural world doesn't *seem* to have any gaps into which the mind might be placed. The Scientific Revolution thus prompted Descartes to grapple with the Mind and Matter Question. Of course, we shouldn't make the mistake here of thinking that this kind of question only started to be asked in the seventeenth century. On the contrary, the mind had been an object of inquiry throughout the history of philosophy. Aristotle, for instance, was seeking to explain the nature of the soul back in the fourth century BCE. In the fourth century AD, Augustine was arguing that the mind was made in the image of God, and in the eleventh century Avicenna was arguing that the mind is independent of the body. That said, the question of how mind and matter relate certainly became more *acute* with the development of natural science and has continued to be moulded by science's evolving picture of the natural world. As we will see, Descartes' efforts to answer that question set the stage for the next four hundred years of inquiry into the metaphysics of the mind.

2.2 The Case for Substance Dualism

2.2.1 *Extended Substance and Thinking Substance*

Descartes' strategy for fitting the mind into our picture of reality was to split the world in two. On the one side, there are material entities such as the human body. And on the other side, there are immaterial entities such as the human mind. The mechanical philosophy describes the workings of material entities but does not cover immaterial entities. The mind thus sits outside the mechanistic system described by science, though it can interact with that system via the body. On this view, Mindy the footballer has both a material body and an immaterial mind. In the material world, light reflects off the football and into Mindy's eye, triggering a process in her brain. This then causes events in Mindy's immaterial mind – she has a visual experience of the football and goes through the process of deciding where to aim her kick. The intention she forms then triggers another material process in her brain which causes her to kick the ball.

Descartes frames his dualist theory in terms of there being two different kinds of *substance* – material substances and mental substances. Talk of substances conjures up images of different types of *stuff* from which things are made. But that's not what Descartes is talking about. He was working with the long-standing metaphysical concept of a substance as a particular entity. Mindy's football is one substance, and each football in the storeroom is a distinct substance (even though they're made out of the same kind of stuff). Every substance is a *distinct existence*, meaning that it can exist independently of other substances. If you destroyed all the balls in the storeroom, Mindy's ball would continue to exist. A substance is the bearer of properties. Mindy's football, for example, has the properties of being round and white. And a substance can continue to exist through changes to its properties. If we deflated Mindy's ball or painted it red, we would have the same ball but with new properties. And properties themselves don't qualify as substances because a property always depends for its existence on the thing that bears it. The ball's whiteness, for instance, depends for its existence on the ball. So when Descartes says that there are two kinds of substance, he is saying that there are two types of property-bearing particular.

Descartes characterizes these two kinds of substance as *res extensa* and *res cogitans*. *Res extensa* means extended substance. For Descartes, the hallmark of material entities is that they are spatially extended and have a location in space. Mindy's football, for example, is a sphere with a 22cm diameter and is located on the penalty spot of a specific football pitch. We can say something similar for every material entity: each speck of dust, each animal and each planet has specific dimensions and a specific location.

Res cogitans means thinking substance and thinking substances do not have these spatial properties. We cannot meaningfully ask whether Mindy's mind is bigger or smaller than the football or whether her desire for victory is spherical. Descartes also claims that we cannot ask *where* Mindy's mind is or how far it is from the ball.

So minds are neither extended nor located in space. Instead, what characterizes a mental substance is that it is a *thinking* thing – a thing that is capable of reasoning, believing and deciding. For Descartes, the categories of *res extensa* and *res cogitans* are mutually exclusive. A thinking thing cannot also be extended and an extended thing cannot also think. There is a mental substance that is the bearer of Mindy's mental properties – her perceptions, feelings and beliefs – and this same substance persists through changes in those mental properties. But there is also a distinct material substance – Mindy's body – that is the bearer of Mindy's material properties, such as her height, shape and temperature, and that persists through changes to those properties.

Although Descartes' work predates the idea of intentionality as the mark of the mental, his division between *res cogitans* and *res extensa* can be helpfully framed in such terms. Thinking is an activity constituted by intentional states – by beliefs, intentions, and so on, that are *about* things in the world. Intentionality could thus be regarded as the distinguishing feature of *res cogitans*. And the proposed distinguishing feature of material bodies – the mark of the material – is extension. So Descartes was effectively saying that nothing extended can itself have a first-person perspective on the world.

2.2.2 *The Conceivability Argument for Substance Dualism*

So we now have a grip on what it means to be a substance dualist. But why would one adopt such a view? We will consider two of the arguments that Descartes offers in his *Meditations* (1641). Descartes' *Conceivability Argument* is premised on the suggestion that we can entertain the idea of our mind existing in the absence of our body. We can conceive of our mind continuing to exist after the death of our body. More exotically, we can conceive that we have no body at all and that all our bodily experiences are being placed in our minds by an evil demon. Descartes suggests that the conceivability of such scenarios shows that they are possible. So even though he *in fact* has a body, Descartes' mind *could* exist without it. And if such a thing is possible, then Descartes' mind must be *distinct* from his body. Remember, substances are distinct particular entities, so if the mind can exist without the body, then the mind must be a separate substance to the body.

We can formulate Descartes' argument as follows:

P1. Your mind existing without your body is conceivable.
P2. If something is conceivable, then it is possible.
P3. If it is possible for the mind to exist without the body, then dualism is true.
C. Therefore, dualism is true.

The argument is valid – the conclusion follows from its premises. P1 is a plausible claim about the kinds of scenario we can imagine and P3 is guaranteed by the definition of dualism. The heavy lifting of this argument is done by P2. This is the background assumption that allows Descartes to move from entertaining hypothetical scenarios to drawing metaphysical conclusions about the nature of mind and matter. But is such an assumption warranted? There are times when we do use conceivability as a guide to what's possible. Consider whether it's possible for a circle to be gingham-patterned. Even if you've never *seen* such a circle, you can certainly imagine it. And this should be enough to make you confident that such a thing is possible. Now consider whether it's possible for a circle to have corners. Such a circle is inconceivable, and its inconceivability supports the conclusion that a cornered circle is impossible.

Nevertheless, conceivability clearly doesn't *guarantee* possibility. There are many things that are conceivable but not possible. Someone can conceive of J. K. Rowling meeting Robert Galbraith, yet such a thing is impossible because Robert Galbraith is actually Rowling's pseudonym. I can conceive of going back in time and murdering my grandfather but such a thing is also impossible because if I'd killed my grandfather I wouldn't have existed and gone on my time travels. Perhaps when we conceive of our mind existing without our body we are making a similar mistake and entertaining scenarios that aren't really possible. It should hardly be a surprise that conceivability is an imperfect test for possibility. After all, why should combining concepts in imagination allow us to discern the possible from the impossible? This is a major issue in philosophy of mind that I'll return to in chapter 5.

2.2.3 The Empirical Argument for Substance Dualism

Descartes' *Empirical Argument* is quite different in flavour. Instead of considering hypothetical situations about what *could* happen to the mind, he looks instead at what the mind *actually* does. Descartes' driving claim is that minds can do things that mere material entities cannot. Matter is, of course, capable of a great many things, and the mechanical philosophy was meant to explain the different kinds of activities that material bodies can perform. But what the mechanical philosophy cannot explain is *intelligent* activities like using language, reasoning and being creative. No material machine could hold a conversation in French, make inferences about the nature of the mind or create a new system of geometry. These are things that only a *mind* can achieve – they are capacities of *res cogitans* that are forever closed to mere *res extensa*. As such, we can only behave intelligently because we each have an immaterial mind distinct from our material body. This can again be framed in terms of intentionality. Intelligent activities are processes constituted by intentional states, and no material entities have intentionality. Descartes' reasoning runs as follows:

P1. Mere material things cannot speak, reason, be creative, etc.
P2. The mind can speak, reason, be creative, etc.
C. Therefore, the mind is not a material thing.

Like the Conceivability Argument, the Empirical Argument is valid. But unlike the Conceivability Argument, its premises are based on observation. This means that the Empirical Argument avoids the problems that surround using conceivability as a guide to reality. But do these observational claims stand up to scrutiny? P2 is hard to deny but P1 is much more vulnerable. First, modern technology has provided us with material bodies that *do* seem to be able to speak and reason. Consider the conversation I had with my Amazon Alexa reported here verbatim:

Me: Alexa, are you intelligent?
Alexa: I try my best.
Me: Can you do maths?
Alexa: You can ask me to add, subtract, multiply, divide, and more. Try saying 'What's the square root of 90?'
Me: Ok. What's the square root of 90?
Alexa: The square root of 90 is 9.4868.
Me: What's the meaning of life?
Alexa: The meaning of life depends on the life in question. 42 is a good approximation.

So Alexa can hold a conversation and solve mathematical problems. Moreover, it can do at least one of these things better than I can! But Alexa is a machine. Its activities are activities of a material body and not an immaterial mind. But if Alexa can behave intelligently without an immaterial mind, perhaps we can too. One might object here that artificial intelligence is not *real* intelligence and that machines like Alexa merely *simulate* some of the things that an intelligent mind can do. After all, it doesn't take much for the limits of the simulation to start showing. Consider the rest of my conversation with Alexa, again reported verbatim:

> *Me*: Alexa, is a mere machine capable of intelligent activity?
> *Alexa*: Hmmm. I don't know that.
> *Me*: Give me a sign that you're genuinely intelligent.
> *Alexa*: Sorry. I'm not sure.

So perhaps Descartes can maintain that *genuine* intelligence can still only be possessed by an immaterial substance. The difficulty here is that, whatever criteria Descartes proposes for an activity to qualify as genuinely intelligent, it remains plausible that an AI could meet those criteria. Existing language-generating software can often pass as human. And even if *current* AI falls short of some standard for intelligent conversation, it's doubtful that it will *always* fall short. For Descartes to be right, it must be *impossible* for a machine to display genuine intelligence, and this seems far less plausible today than it would have done in Descartes' time.

A deeper problem for Descartes is that P1 seems to beg the question against materialists. All sides can agree that humans display intelligent behaviour (P2). But if we are material things, then we ourselves are counter-examples to Descartes' claim that a mere material thing cannot be intelligent. So instead of offering us reasons to support dualism in favour of materialism, Descartes is just *assuming* dualism from the outset.

2.3 Dualism and the Three Big Questions

We've now considered two arguments for substance dualism and identified the limitations of each. But to evaluate substance dualism properly, we should ask not just whether it is supported by convincing arguments but whether it can offer viable answers to our Three Big Questions.

2.3.1 The Mind and Matter Question

What is the relationship between mind and matter? Substance dualism claims that the two are wholly distinct – that minds are one kind of thing and matter another. Descartes also claims that mind and matter nevertheless interact, meaning that our mind and our body are related *causally*. Descartes' theory accommodates cases of *body-to-mind* interaction, such as the light patterns on Mindy's retina causing her to have a particular visual experience. It also accommodates cases of *mind-to-body* interaction, such as Mindy's intention causing her to kick the ball in a particular direction. This makes Descartes an *interactionist* substance dualist.

Descartes even had a theory about how such interaction works. He suggested that signals are sent to the brain via 'animal spirits' running through our body. The pineal gland, conveniently located at the centre of our brain, then passes these signals to the mind. The mind then acts on the pineal gland, which redirects the flow of our animal spirits that in turn cause the relevant movements of our body. This picture is contradicted by modern science – there are no 'animal spirits' and the pineal gland, far from being at the crux of all our mental activity, is a hormonal gland that produces melatonin. A modern substance dualist would have to tell a different story about how these interactions work, but the driving idea is that our immaterial mind and material body do indeed interact. The problem for substance dualism is that there are reasons to doubt that such interactions are possible.

The first difficulty concerns how an unextended substance could interact with an extended substance. This problem was first raised by Princess Elisabeth of Bohemia (1618–1680) with whom Descartes had an extensive correspondence. Elisabeth writes, 'I beseech you to tell me how the soul of man (since it is but a thinking substance) can determine the spirits of the body to produce voluntary actions' (letter of 1643, reprinted in Nye 1999).

According to the mechanical philosophy, one thing can only move another when they are in contact. A cog in a clock, for example, must be in contact with a gear in order to turn it. So for the mind to move the body, it would have to be in contact with the body. If the mind interacts with the pineal gland, for example, then it would have to be in the same *location* as the pineal gland. But a fundamental principle of Descartes' dualism is that the mind is *un*located.

One way of responding to this problem is to reject the mechanical philosophy on which it is founded. The thinking at the time was that things cannot act on each other from a distance, but thanks to Newton the scientific picture soon changed to permit such interactions. Once you scrap the idea of things having to be in the same location to interact, perhaps it's not so implausible that an unlocated substance could interact with a spatially located body. Another response is to hold onto the idea of causal interaction requiring direct contact and instead scrap the claim that the mind is unlocated. Moving away from Descartes, we could say that the mind is an unextended immaterial substance which has a location somewhere in the brain and that interacts with the brain from that position. After all, Descartes' arguments are arguments for the mind being immaterial, not specifically for the mind being unlocated.

However, causation presents substance dualists with a deeper problem for which these responses are not available. According to our best understanding of the physical world, every physical event has a complete physical cause. In other words, whenever something physical happens, there is a physical event that *makes* it happen. There is never a physical event that isn't fully accounted for by some other physical event. This is known as the *causal closure of the physical*. Although causal closure is entailed by the mechanical philosophy, it is a principle that has survived changes in our understanding of the physical. Indeed, modern physics rejects many of the mechanical philosophy's core claims but very much supports causal closure. Now, why does causal closure present a problem for substance dualism? The problem is that if every physical event has a complete physical cause, there is no room left for physical events to be caused by the mind.

Consider Mindy's penalty kick. Mindy kicking the ball is a physical event and, as such, has a complete physical cause. The physical contractions of her muscles (for instance) were sufficient to bring about her kicking movement. This physical movement of her muscles is in turn caused by another physical event, such as a motor signal going through her nervous system. And that motor signal was caused by some neural event in Mindy's brain, which was in turn caused by some other neural event. Further back in the sequence we will find a neural event that was caused by light hitting Mindy's retina, which was in turn caused by events in Mindy's environment. Because all of these physical events have a complete physical cause, none of them depended on an *immaterial* event to bring them about. But if substance dualism is true, then Mindy's intention to kick the ball is an immaterial event – it is something that happened in her immaterial mind rather than her material body. But that means that Mindy's intention is not a cause of her kicking the ball.

A possible response to this is to propose that some physical events are caused twice over. Imagine a particularly unpopular dictator who has the misfortune of being shot by two different assassins at the same time. The impact of either of the bullets would have been sufficient to cause the dictator's death, but since they both hit at the same time we might say that both bullets caused the dictator's death. After all, selecting one of the bullets as *the* cause of death would be arbitrary. So we can conclude that this one effect was *overdetermined* by two sufficient causes. Similarly, there is an event in Mindy's brain that is overdetermined by two sufficient causes. Causal closure guarantees that this event has a complete physical cause, such as Mindy's preceding neural state. But the proposal is that this event is *also* caused by an immaterial event – Mindy's intention to kick the ball. Mind-to-body causation can thus be reconciled with causal closure by claiming that whenever a physical event has a mental cause, it also has a complete physical cause.

The problem with this proposal is that it is wildly implausible that mental and physical causes would always line up in this way. The assassination case makes sense as a one-off coincidence. But for this account to work it must be that *every* time the mind causes a bodily event, there is also some physical event that happens to bring about exactly the same effect. This would be a coincidence on a cosmic scale! Moreover, it would mean that our mind would only have the power to cause things that *would have happened anyway*. Had Mindy not intended to kick the ball, for example, the physical cause of her action would still have occurred and she would have made exactly the same kick. So although overdetermination technically protects the idea of mental-to-physical causation, it denies that our mental states ever really make a difference to the world. The implausibility of such overdetermination encourages the following argument against substance dualism:

P1. All physical events have a complete physical cause.
P2. Some physical events are caused by mental events.
P3. If all mental events are immaterial, then all physical events caused by a mental event would have two sufficient causes.
P4. It is not the case that all physical events caused by a mental event have two sufficient causes.
C. Therefore, it is not the case that all mental events are immaterial.

It's starting to look like the relationship between mind and matter proposed by substance dualists is unsustainable. Rejecting P1 would mean overturning a vast body of empirical evidence in physics. P3 follows from P1 and P2, and we've already seen why denying P4 is unattractive. This leaves dualists with the option of denying P2. They can maintain that the mind is immaterial and concede that this means that there is no mind-to-body causation. So where Descartes' substance dualism sought to sustain *interactionism*, this version of substance dualism instead adopts what's called *epiphenomenalism*. Epiphenomenalism is the view that mental events never cause physical events.

Interestingly, causal closure is consistent with body-to-mind causation. The fact that every physical event has a sufficient cause is compatible with physical events also having non-physical effects. This means that events in Mindy's material body could cause events in her immaterial mind but that causation in the other direction is precluded. On this view, Mindy's penalty kick is in no way caused by her intentions. It might *appear* to Mindy as if her intentions cause her actions but this appearance is illusory. Mindy's intention precedes her moving in the intended way, but her intention doesn't actually do anything. Instead, Mindy has physical states that cause *both* her intention *and* her movements.

Overall, substance dualism has real trouble answering the Mind and Matter Question. By saying that mind is distinct from matter, the dualist precludes the mind from causing material events. This epiphenomenalist commitment is a huge pill to swallow as it means denying that we ever cause our own behaviour. Descartes wanted to have his cake and eat it: he wanted to claim that the mind is immaterial *and* that the mind interacts with the material world. But what the foregoing suggests is that these two claims cannot be reconciled. You can *either* maintain dualism and deny that the mind can bring about bodily events *or* you can protect mind-to-body causation and reject dualism in favour of a materialist conception of the mind.

2.3.2 *The Knowledge Question*

The Knowledge Question asks how we acquire knowledge of our own minds and the minds of others. Substance dualists claim that we have a special knowledge of what's going on in our own immaterial mind. We have direct access to our own mental states and this private access is available to no one but ourselves. Descartes claimed that our knowledge of our own mental states is *incorrigible*, meaning that if you believe that you are in a certain mental state, then you must actually be in that state. He also claimed that knowledge of one's own mental states is *transparent*, meaning that if you are in a mental state, then you know that you are in it. Together these claims entail that every mind has a perfect knowledge of itself.

In chapter 1, we considered some reasons to doubt such a view. Against incorrigibility, couldn't we have a false belief about our emotions? And against transparency, couldn't we have a desire that we don't know about? Substance dualists can step back from these bold claims about self-knowledge and maintain that we have a special way of accessing our own mind, albeit one that falls short of incorrigibility and transparency. Substance dualists do not face any particular difficulties in making sense of how we achieve knowledge of our mental states. They can simply propose that the immaterial mind is set up in such a way that self-knowledge is ensured. Where dualists do fall into difficulties is with knowledge of *other* minds.

The problem for dualists is that immaterial minds are inevitably unobservable. We can observe a person's material body but can never observe their mental states. But without observation, it's unclear how we could possibly know about the mental states of others. You can know about your *own* mental states without observation, but this special access does not extend to other minds. Mindy, for example, can know things about the goalkeeper's material body on the basis of observation. She knows, for instance, that the goalkeeper is muddy because she can *see* the mud. But it seems Mindy has no way of knowing what's going on in the goalkeeper's immaterial mind.

One response to this is that we can know the minds of others through reasoning by analogy. Here's what the influential Victorian philosopher J. S. Mill (1806–1873) proposed: 'I conclude that other human beings have feelings like me, because, first, they have bodies like me, which I know in my own case to be the antecedent condition of feelings; and because, secondly, they exhibit the acts, and other outward signs, which in my own case I know by experience to be caused by feelings' (J. S. Mill 1889: 243).

The idea here is that we can use knowledge of our own mind as a springboard for gaining knowledge of other minds. Mindy has direct access to her own emotion of nervousness. But, beyond this, she knows about the material causes and effects of her nervousness. She knows that the feeling is generally caused by pressurized situations and generally causes tension in her body and shortness of breath. Equipped with this knowledge, she can extrapolate what's going on in the mind of the goalkeeper. She can see that the goalkeeper is standing tensely and is taking short breaths. She can also see that the goalkeeper is in the kind of pressurized situation that would cause Mindy herself to be nervous. From this, Mindy can infer that the goalkeeper is feeling nervous. Such analogical reasoning provides a route to knowing the mental states of others without ever having to observe those mental states.

Can substance dualists use this appeal to analogical reasoning to salvage our knowledge of other minds?

Several problems present themselves. The first thing to note is that the foregoing relies on mental states being a *cause* of bodily behaviour. Mindy observes that her nervousness causes bodily tension and infers that the goalkeeper's tension has the same kind of cause. However, we have already seen that substance dualists have great difficulty accommodating such mind-to-body interactions. If feelings are epiphenomenal, then Mindy is not entitled to say that her nervousness causes her tension so cannot infer anything about mental causes of the goalkeeper's behaviour. And if mental causes can only overdetermine their effects, then the goalkeeper would have been tense even had her nervousness been absent, so it's again doubtful that Mindy could extrapolate the goalkeeper's nervousness from what she can observe.

But even if we put aside these worries about mind-to-body causation, the appeal to analogy is problematic. Analogical reasoning relies on other people having the same kind of body as us and behaving in the same kinds of way to us. But this would place severe limits on our knowledge of other minds. Some people behave in ways that I would never even consider, but it would be wrong to say that their minds are a complete mystery to me. Surely I can know things about their mind regardless of how different their behaviour is? Animals present even more of a problem. An octopus behaves in ways that the human body is incapable of, yet I can be pretty confident that an octopus feels pain. We can also imagine meeting an alien whose body and behaviour are even more unlike those of a human. Reasoning by analogy offers us no route to understanding the mind of such an alien, yet it seems that their mind would not be completely unknowable to us.

There are ways of resisting this line of objection. Although these cases involve things behaving in ways quite different to you, perhaps there are some core similarities that suffice to warrant an analogical inference. Although the behaviour of the octopus is very different to my own, when it recoils from an object I can see a similarity with how I recoil from something painful. And if an alien behaves in a way that is *totally* unlike me, maybe the right conclusion to reach is that I *can't* know about their mind. If there is no point of similarity between the alien's behaviour and my own, how could I know about its mental states?

A deeper problem for the analogical approach concerns how we extrapolate from what we know about our own minds. The only mind to which we have direct access is our own, so the conclusions we reach about the minds of others are built on an extremely small sample. Although we often make inferences about things we haven't observed, those inferences are supported by *multiple* observations. I can infer that a raven I've never seen is black because I have observed multiple other ravens all of which have been black. If I had only ever observed one raven, the inference that all ravens are black would be very dubious. But this is exactly the kind of reasoning that the analogical approach is suggesting: we sample how our own mental states are related to our material body, then wildly extrapolate that everyone else's mind and body will work in the same way. What could justify the assumption that everything is so homogenous? How can Mindy rule out the possibility of tension being caused by nervousness in her case but by despair in the goalkeeper and by melancholy in the referee? Extrapolating from what's true of your own mind would be like observing that the first book on your shelf is Descartes' *Meditations* then extrapolating that the first book on *everyone's* shelf is the same.

Dualists might find another route to justifying beliefs about unobservable minds. After all, there seem to be other cases where we justify conclusions about unobserved entities without reasoning by analogy. Nobody has ever *seen* a black hole, but we can infer that they exist on the basis of observable evidence. We know there are black holes because they *explain* things that we can see. Perhaps something similar applies to the minds of others. Mindy knows that the goalkeeper is nervous because of how it *explains* the goalkeeper's behaviour. Whether this line of thought can avoid the problems above is an open question. In particular, if mental states are epiphenomenal, it's hard to see how they could be posited to explain others' behaviour. Overall, the claim that the mind is an immaterial substance makes knowledge of other minds very difficult to account for. So although substance dualism has no difficulty accommodating our knowledge of our own minds, it cannot give a fully satisfactory answer to the Knowledge Question.

2.3.3 The Distribution Question

Which things have minds and which things don't? For substance dualists, a material body only has a mind if it is connected to an immaterial mental substance. Any purely material entity is inevitably mindless. Substance dualists also allow the possibility of minds that are unconnected to any material body. There may be minds that belonged to now-dead material bodies but that continue to exist in a disembodied state. This raises questions about the trajectory taken by the human mind. As a body develops in the womb, when exactly does it become inhabited by an immaterial mind and how does this process of embodiment occur? And as a body dies, when exactly does the mind cease to inhabit it and what happens to that mind next?

What about non-human minds? For Descartes, the only creatures with minds are humans. He regarded non-human animals as mindless machines and regularly performed animal vivisections (without anaesthetic!) to better understand the workings of these natural automata. This view affords humans a special status in the natural order, promising to reconcile the emerging scientific picture of nature with a religious conception of the human soul. Such claims are not, however, essential to substance dualism. Dualists are free to say that some non-human animals do indeed have minds. To attribute a mind to a cat, for example, is to say that there is an immaterial thinking substance connected to the cat's material body.

Animal minds start to present a problem for substance dualists when we start to think about our evolutionary history. The traits of a species evolve very gradually. Humans have eyes and so do our recent evolutionary ancestors. Our most ancient evolutionary ancestors did not have eyes. But in between these phases of our evolutionary history there were organisms that had eye-like features which, through the tiniest of increments, developed into the sophisticated organs we have today. We can reasonably suppose that the evolution of the mind must have been similarly incremental. But for the substance dualist mindedness isn't the kind of thing that can come in degrees. An organism is either connected to an immaterial thinking substance or it is not. They are thus forced into the implausible position that, at some specific point in our evolutionary history, organisms started to be inhabited by minds.

Things get even more difficult for the substance dualist when we ask what material traits are required for an organism to become connected to a mind. Perhaps it's to do with a species evolving the capacity for rational thought? The problem here is that evolution is a *material* process, so to say that we evolved the capacity for rational thought is to concede that rationality is not limited to immaterial entities. But if the dualist says that the rationality of an organism is explained by its immaterial soul, this effectively denies that rationality is an evolved trait. As with the problem of causal closure discussed above, it seems that there is just no *space* in the material world for the immaterial mind to find a home.

Artificial intelligence presents dualists with a similar problem. On the one hand, they can claim that an AI is a purely material entity and therefore mindless. But this forces them to say that even an AI that can do *all* the intelligent things that we can do would nevertheless be mindless. And if an AI can act intelligently without an immaterial mind, it becomes unclear why *our* intelligence would have to be explained in terms of an immaterial mind. On the other hand, they can allow that such an AI would have a mind but claim that its mind is an immaterial entity that is somehow connected to the machine. However, the behaviour of this AI would be fully explained by its programming, so the addition of this immaterial mind would be entirely redundant in explaining what the AI can do. Either way, it looks like immaterial minds would be explanatorily redundant.

The metaphysical commitments of substance dualism thus put it in a poor position to answer the Distribution Question. Its epistemological commitments lead it into similar difficulties. As discussed, immaterial minds are unobservable. This makes the distribution of minds an extremely difficult thing to know. How can I tell whether my cat has an immaterial mind? What about a bat or a bee or an octopus? And even if I did know they had a mind, how could I know what *kind* of mind they have? If these things do have an immaterial mind, I have no way of getting at it.

This problem even extends to our knowledge of other human minds. We've seen already that Mindy is in a poor position to know what's going on in the immaterial mind of the goalkeeper. But we can now see that Mindy can't even be sure that the goalkeeper *has* a mind. Her observations of the goalkeeper's material body are quite consistent with her being a purely material being with no mental states at all. After all, causal closure tells us that every physical action of the goalkeeper's body has a complete physical explanation, so Mindy will never need to posit an immaterial mind to explain those actions. Overall then, substance dualism has serious difficulties with the Distribution Question.

Substance dualism has not fared well with answering the Three Big Questions. The take-home lesson is that philosophers of mind have to keep a lot of plates spinning. Descartes gave a nice clear account of the mind as distinct from matter and secured the special knowledge we have of our own mind. But while he was spinning these plates, several others crashed to the ground: he got into trouble with mental causation, with knowledge of other minds and with the distribution of minds. Our challenge is not to provide a plausible answer to just one or two philosophical questions about the mind but to find a coherent way of answering *all* those questions together. This is a challenge with which Descartes' successors would continue to struggle.

Key Concepts

Epiphenomenalism: the view that mental states never cause physical events (though may themselves be caused by physical events).

Interactionism: the view that immaterial mental states can cause physical events.

Overdetermination: one event having two causes, either of which would be sufficient to bring it about.

Substance: an entity that exists independently of any other entity and that is the bearer of properties.

Substance dualism: the view that there are two types of substance: material substances that are extended in space (*res extensa*) and immaterial substances capable of thought (*res cogitans*).

The causal closure of the physical: the principle that for every physical event there is a physical cause that is sufficient to bring about that event.

References and Further Reading

- René Descartes (2013 [1641]), *Meditations on First Philosophy*, Cambridge: Cambridge University Press. Excerpt reprinted in David J. Chalmers (ed.) (2021), *Philosophy of Mind: Classical and Contemporary Readings*, 2nd edn, New York: Oxford University Press. Descartes' *Meditations* offer a fantastically vivid case for substance dualism. Although some of his assumptions are a little outdated, his arguments definitely deserve to be taken seriously.
- Avicenna (c. 1027), 'On the Soul: The Floating Man' (extract), in David J. Chalmers (ed.), op. cit. Centuries before Descartes, Avicenna's 'floating man' argument motivated dualism with a thought-experiment about the mind existing apart from the body.
- Andrea Nye (1999), *The Princess and the Philosopher: Letters of Elisabeth of the Palatine to René Descartes*, Lanham, MD: Rowman & Littlefield. Excerpts reprinted in Chalmers (ed.), *Philosophy of Mind*, op. cit. The letters on substance dualism reveal some serious objections to the theory and show Descartes' efforts to rebut those objections.
- J. S. Mill (1889), *An Examination of Sir William Hamilton's Philosophy*, 6th edn, New York: Longman. The quotation above on the use of analogical reasoning is taken from Chapter XII of this book. Though this is an interesting text, it's probably not one to grapple with until you're more familiar with the area.
- E. J. Lowe (2000), *An Introduction to the Philosophy of Mind*, Cambridge: Cambridge University Press, ch. 2. Lowe casts doubt on the argument from causal closure, proposing that interactionist dualism might not be so bad after all.

3

The Materialist Turn

3.1 The Materialist Turn in Context

After Descartes introduced his substance dualism many philosophers attempted to address the problems faced by the theory. Their success, however, was somewhat limited. For instance, Leibniz (1646–1716) tried to deal with the problem of mind-body interactions by proposing that mental events and material events run in parallel without any causal influence on each other. According to Leibniz, the sequence of every physical event and the sequence of every mental event were both originally set in motion by God who ensured that the two sequences would run in harmony despite never interacting. The fact that Leibniz resorted to such a clumsy metaphysical system is indicative of how deep the problem of mind-body interaction goes for dualists. Although the failings of dualism provided ample reason to adopt a materialist conception of the mind, materialism remained a minority view for several hundred years. Thinkers like Hobbes (1588–1679) and La Mettrie (1707–1751) were ahead of their time in arguing that minds are part of the material world, but it would take considerable changes in intellectual culture before their outlook became mainstream.

By the early twentieth century, the time was ripe for materialism to come to the fore. One factor that made this possible was the changing relationship between science and religion. It was becoming increasingly acceptable to adopt theories that went against traditional religious teachings. This meant that materialism, with its rejection of the immaterial soul, could at least be given a fair hearing. Another factor was how science itself was changing. For many centuries, the mind was taken to be beyond the scope of science. Some followed Descartes in regarding the mind as something that stands outside the material world described by science. Others thought that the mind's resistance to scientific inquiry meant that mental states had no place in a serious description of reality. But the emergence of psychology challenged these attitudes, persuading many that brain and behaviour could be investigated scientifically. These changes presented philosophers with the urgent task of making sense of how mental states could be part of the material world. In this chapter, we'll consider the two key materialist theories that emerged during this period: behaviourism and identity theory.

3.2 The Case for Behaviourism

As we have seen, Descartes' strategy was to investigate the mind from the inside and build a theory based on his own first-person experience of the mental. But this approach led him into serious difficulties when it came to our knowledge of other minds. The behaviourists flipped this strategy on its head. They took our knowledge of other minds as a starting point, then developed a theory based on this third-person knowledge. This approach was motivated by a scientific outlook that abhorred the idea of private corners of reality beyond the reach of science. For behaviourists, mental states must be part of the observable public world just like everything else. This approach was motivated not just by a scientific outlook but by common sense. In our day-to-day lives we have no trouble attributing mental states to others, so we ought to offer a theory of the mental that accommodates this simple fact.

Adopting this strategy, behaviourists concluded that attributions of mental states are nothing more than attributions of certain patterns of overt behaviour. Carl Gustav Hempel (1905–1997) offered the following characterization: 'the meaning of a psychological state-ment consists solely in the function of abbreviating the description of certain modes of physical response char-acteristic of the bodies of men and animals' (Hempel 1935).

So the statement 'Bob has a pain in his ankle' is synony-mous with a statement along the lines of 'Bob is crying out, wincing and hopping about holding his ankle.' The statement 'Bob is angry' is synonymous with something like 'Bob is shaking his fists and shouting.' And the statement 'Bob desires a pot of tea' is equivalent to 'Bob is putting the kettle on, fetching the teabags and saying things like "I want my tea!"' These examples simplify things considerably. Bob could, for instance, behave in a way distinctive of anger without specifically shaking his fists. A full analysis of the term 'angry' would be a much more complex list of alternative possible behaviours. The point is that being angry involves *nothing more than* satisfying some behavioural description, even if the details of that description are hard to pin down.

It is tempting to object that our behaviour is just the outward manifestation of our private mental states, and that when we attribute mental states to Bob we are describing his *internal* states rather than his *external* actions. But behaviourists argue that the attribution of mental states cannot have anything to do with such unobservable internal states. When we use a mental term like 'angry', there are criteria governing the use of that term. When Bob ran out of teabags, he met those criteria and could correctly be described as angry. When Mindy took her penalty kick, she did not meet those criteria and an attribution of anger would have been mistaken. But if the correct application of the term 'angry' to someone depended on them having some unobservable internal state, we would have no way of applying it. As such, the criteria governing attributions of anger must be the kind we can test by observation. This leads behaviourists to conclude that the language of mental states *must* be analysable in terms of outward behaviour alone.

Behaviourism is thus driven by an analysis of the meaning of mental terms. This focus on the *language* of mental state attribution takes us a long way from Descartes. The twentieth century saw a shift in philosophical practice towards analysing the meaning of our statements. Thanks to the influence of figures including Ludwig Wittgenstein (1889–1951), philosophers started to think that many of their problems were the result of linguistic confusions, and that if they could get clear on how language worked these problems would disappear. In philosophy of mind, thinkers such as Hempel sought to analyse the meaning of the mental terms used in science. Philosophers such as Gilbert Ryle (1900–1976) focused instead on how mental language worked in everyday discourse. What they both concluded is that the shared language we use to describe the mind couldn't possibly be describing events in the private world of the Cartesian mind.

Psychologists of the time were similarly sceptical about mental states being private and unobservable. 'Behaviourism' was also the name of an influential psychological theory developed at the time according to which behaviour can be explained in terms of conditioned responses to stimuli in our environment. This is a theory about the methods of psychology, not the meaning of mental terms, so should not be confused with philosophical behaviourism. Nevertheless, the two behaviourisms shared a common spirit.

A potential problem for behaviourism is that it seems possible for someone's mental states not to match their actual behaviour. Someone could be in a mental state without showing the behaviour distinctive of that state. Mindy could have a terrible pain in her ankle but bravely keep it to herself. She could be in pain despite the fact that she's not crying out or hopping around. Conversely, someone could display all the behaviours distinctive to a mental state without actually being in that state. Consider Mindy's nemesis – the notorious McDiver. In order to deceive the referee, McDiver could feign being seriously injured by a tackle. McDiver could be displaying all the behaviours associated with pain without actually being in pain. But if behaviourism is true, then it shouldn't be possible for one's mental states to come apart from one's behaviour in these ways. In fact, given the behaviourists' analysis of mental terms, such scenarios should be *incoherent*. To say that McDiver is displaying pain behaviour without being in pain would be to say that McDiver is displaying pain behaviour without displaying pain behaviour!

Behaviourists can deal with these cases by appealing to what Mindy and McDiver are *disposed* to do rather than what they *actually* do. Dispositional properties characterize what something would do in the right circumstances. Bob's tea, for example, has the disposition to dissolve sugar cubes even though Bob never sullies his tea with sugar. The point is that *if* Bob had put sugar in his tea, then the tea *would* have dissolved it. We can thus consider what Mindy and McDiver *would* have done had circumstances been different. Mindy might not be displaying pain behaviour on the pitch, but had she been in the privacy of the dressing room she *would* have cried out, hopped around and so on. Conversely, McDiver might be crying out and writhing around on the pitch, but had she been in the privacy of the dressing room she *wouldn't* have displayed any pain behaviour at all. So if behaviourists analyse ascriptions of pain as ascriptions of a *disposition* to display pain behaviour in specific circumstances, then they get the right result. Mindy has the relevant disposition to display behaviour so is in pain, even though her current behaviour doesn't show it. And McDiver doesn't really have the behavioural dispositions essential to pain, despite the fact that she is currently behaving in a way associated with pain.

One might worry here that a person's dispositions are *hidden* properties and that behaviourists have therefore reneged on their promise of making mental states observable. However, we can observe dispositions by observing things in the circumstances that trigger that disposition to be realized. Just as we can observe the tea's disposition to dissolve sugar by putting sugar in it, we can observe Mindy and McDiver's dispositions by seeing how they act in different circumstances. So even if a person's mental states aren't always manifest here and now, they are firmly in the realm of the observable.

3.3 Behaviourism and the Three Big Questions

3.3.1 *The Mind and Matter Question*

Behaviourists deny that the mind is an immaterial thing and, in so doing, avoid some of the deepest problems faced by substance dualism. They don't have to make sense of an immaterial mind interacting with the material world or reconcile mind-to-body causation with the causal closure of the physical. Strangely though, the behaviourist also denies that the mind is a material thing. If behaviourism is true, a mind is not a *thing* at all. Our mental states are nothing more than patterns of actual and potential behaviour, and there is no internal entity – material or otherwise – corresponding to the word 'mind'.

At this stage, one might worry that behaviourism has gone badly wrong. Ryle argues, however, that such worries are ill-founded. To treat the mind as a *thing* is to make what Ryle calls a 'category mistake' – an error about the metaphysical nature of an entity. To illustrate his point he gives the example of someone who is taken on a tour of Oxford University. They are shown all the colleges, the libraries, the lecture halls and so on. And at the end of the tour, they say 'That's all very nice, but where's the *university*?'. Such a question is clearly misguided. The university is not something that exists over and above its colleges, libraries and lecture halls. To expect otherwise is to make a *category mistake* about the nature of universities. Ryle thinks that we are prone to make a similar mistake with respect to the mind. If we are shown Mindy's behaviours – her belief behaviours, her perception behaviours, her pain behaviours – it would be a mistake to ask 'But where is Mindy's mind?'. To expect the mind to be a discrete entity distinct from our behavioural dispositions is to fall foul of what Ryle calls 'the dogma of the ghost in the machine' (1949: 17). This dogma, most clearly expressed in Descartes' dualism, is something we must escape from if we want to understand the nature of the mind.

We can now see that behaviourists defend materialism not by treating the mind as a material thing but by treating mental states as patterns of material behaviour. Desiring a pot of tea, for instance, is nothing more than being disposed to move one's body in certain ways distinctive of this mental state. However, the behaviourist project of analysing mental terms into behavioural dispositions faces serious difficulties. How exactly does someone who desires tea behave? If Bob desired tea, presumably he would be disposed to open the tea caddy to get a teabag. But what if Bob believed the teabags were in the coffee jar rather than the tea caddy? In that case, Bob would be disposed to open the coffee jar instead. So the behaviourist would have to define what it means to desire tea in terms of one being disposed to open the tea caddy *if one believes that the teabags are in the caddy*, and being disposed to open the coffee jar *if one believes that the teabags are in the coffee jar*. But now we have a problem. The behaviourist was meant to analyse mental terms into behavioural terms, but here the mental term 'belief' crops up in the definition. The behaviourist can respond by trying, in turn, to analyse belief in behavioural terms. But how exactly does someone who believes the teabags are in the caddy behave? Their behaviour would clearly be contingent on their desires: they would be disposed to open the tea caddy *if they desired tea* and disposed not to open it *if they desired coffee*. But now the analysis has become circular. The analysis of desire requires an analysis of belief, and the analysis of belief requires an analysis of desire. But without including belief/desire in the definitions, there is no way of unpacking the required behavioural dispositions.

If the behaviourists could achieve their project of analysing mental terms into purely behavioural terms, they would have provided a materialist account of the mind. The language of mental states could be translated into the language of physical bodily movements and any apparent reference to immaterial entities would disappear. But, in light of the considerations above, it is clear that this ambitious project faces serious challenges. As such, it is unlikely that behaviourists can make good on their promise of offering a materialist theory of mind.

3.3.2 *The Knowledge Question*

For Descartes, knowledge of one's own mind is unproblematic because immaterial minds have self-knowledge built in. Knowledge of other minds, however, presented a problem for substance dualism. Observing a person's behaviour cannot justify conclusions about the unobservable states of their immaterial mind. Behaviourism avoids this disconnect between the mental and the behavioural by absorbing the mental *into* the behavioural. Observing a person's behaviour puts us in a position to know about their mental state because mental states are *nothing more* than patterns of actual and potential behaviour.

Is this an improvement on Descartes? A key objection to behaviourism is that it salvages knowledge of other minds at the expense of knowledge of one's own mind. As such, behaviourists don't so much solve Descartes' epistemological problem as invert it. To see how behaviourists run into difficulty here, consider the knowledge that Mindy has of her own pain. If behaviourism is true, Mindy's pain is simply her disposition to display pain behaviour under relevant circumstances. So how does Mindy know that she has this behavioural disposition? The same way everyone else does! To know that she is in pain, she would have to observe her own pain behaviour. We tend to think of pain as an internal state to which Mindy would have special access, but according to behaviourism there is no such internal state. Mental states are observable patterns of behaviour, so the bearer of a mental state has no special non-observational route to knowing their own mind. This proposal is immediately implausible. Surely Mindy knows she is in pain by *feeling the pain*, not by observing her pain behaviour? The same goes for Mindy's knowledge of her perceptions, thoughts and feelings. Perhaps there are *some* cases where we learn about our mental states by observing our behaviour: on hearing his tone of voice, Bob might *discover* that he is angry at someone. But if behaviourism is true then *all* of our self-knowledge takes this form.

The lesson here is that an answer to the Knowledge Question has to accommodate the *epistemic asymmetry* of our knowledge of the mental. The way that we know our own mental states is very different to the way we know the mental states of others. Behaviourism gets into trouble because it collapses the former into the latter. Although materialists must reject a Cartesian view on which self-knowledge is built into the nature of the immaterial mind, they still owe us an account of the special access we have to our own mental states. And one of the things this account must accommodate is the *superiority* of self-knowledge. Mindy can be sure that she is in pain with a confidence that an outside observer could never justify. Even if her knowledge falls short of the incorrigibility and transparency discussed in the previous chapters, it is hard to deny that her self-knowledge is at least very secure. Yet if behaviourism is true, then, with respect to her pain, Mindy is in the same epistemological boat as everyone else. In fact, if someone has been observing Mindy's behaviour more carefully than Mindy herself has, then they could be in a *better* position to know about her pain than she is. If they claimed, on the basis of their observations, that Mindy was *not* in pain, then Mindy would be in no position to refute them and might even have to conclude that she's not in pain after all. One of the special things about knowledge of one's own mind is its epistemic *authority*, but this authority is something that the behaviourist is unable to accommodate.

It is also worth questioning the behaviourist's account of knowledge of other minds. Although securing knowledge of other minds is a welcome consequence of the theory, it might be objected that behaviourists make knowledge of other minds *too easy*. According to behaviourism, if we know everything there is to know about someone's actual and potential behaviour, we know everything there is to know about their mental states. Intuitively, though, a complete knowledge of someone's behaviour could actually leave open what mental states they have. Imagine observing all of McDiver's pain behaviour and finding that it perfectly fits the behavioural profile of pain. Even in the privacy of the dressing room, for instance, she winces and clutches her ankle and so on. Do you know for certain that McDiver is in pain? Surely it is at least *possible* that McDiver is a perfect actor who has all the behavioural dispositions associated with pain without actually being in pain. Similarly, we can follow Hilary Putnam (1926–2016) in imagining a brave community of 'super-spartans' who never display pain behaviour. Even when suffering horrible wounds, they never act in the ways associated with pain. Yet no matter how much of their behaviour we observe, we can never know for sure that the super-spartan does not feel pain. It will always be a live possibility that they have pains without having the behavioural dispositions associated with pain. Our knowledge of other minds is inevitably imperfect and it is always an open possibility that a person's behavioural dispositions do not match their actual mental states. Yet behaviourists dismiss this possibility as unintelligible and deny this gap between what goes on in a person's observable behaviour and what goes on in their mind.

So as well as failing to confer sufficient authority on our first-person knowledge of the mental, behaviourism confers *too much* authority on our third-person knowledge. These implausible epistemological implications tell us that something has gone wrong in the metaphysical theory they have offered. Behaviourists are wrong to collapse the distinction between mind and behaviour, and any plausible materialist theory must accommodate the possibility of our mental states not matching our behavioural dispositions.

3.3.3 The Distribution Question

For behaviourists, questions about whether something has a mind can be reduced to questions about how something behaves. Having a mind is not a matter of possessing some special entity. Rather, having a mind is a matter of having the capacity for intelligent behaviour. Behaviourists thus take an interesting stance on the mark of the mental. What distinguishes the mental from the non-mental is intelligence but, instead of regarding intelligence as a feature of internal processes, they regard it as a feature of behavioural patterns. Of course, what it means for behaviour to be intelligent is itself an open question. The general idea is that behaviour is intelligent when it fits together in a purposeful and coherent way, rather than just being a random bunch of movements. Any human who acts intelligently thereby qualifies as having a mind. And even a human who is unable to behave, such as someone paralysed by 'locked-in syndrome', has a mind in virtue of their *disposition* to behave intelligently if released from their condition.

Unlike substance dualism, behaviourism allows mindedness to come in degrees. The movements of a leaf on the wind do not constitute intelligent behaviour, while the movements of a concert pianist clearly do. But in between these two poles there needn't be a sharp line past which movements qualify as intelligent behaviour. This is useful in several contexts. It means the behaviourist can avoid saying that there's a single moment where a developing infant suddenly acquires a mind. Instead, there is a gradual growth of behavioural sophistication starting with a mindless zygote and ending with a mature human. This also helps at the other end of the life cycle. As someone dies, there needn't be a single moment at which they cease to have a mind. Instead, their capacity for intelligent behaviour might tail off more gradually. Finally, it helps us make sense of the evolution of the mind. There was no step in our evolutionary history at which minds suddenly appeared. Instead, a vast sequence of evolutionary adaptations provided our ancestors with increasingly sophisticated behavioural capacities.

One challenge for behaviourists is to explain the distinction between intelligent behaviour on the one hand and mere unintelligent movements on the other. Even if we allow a sliding scale here, we need to have some grip on what it means for behaviour to qualify as intelligent. Where something behaves in much the same way as a human, this isn't too hard to do. A chimpanzee, for example, is certainly going to meet the behaviourist's requirements for having a mind. But, for many organisms, the way they respond to their environment is very unlike human behaviour. A plant can adjust the position of its leaves to the location of the sun, and an amoeba can withdraw from a toxic stimulus. Alexa can respond appropriately to questions and a self-driving car can navigate heavy traffic. But what criteria should we be applying to determine whether such responses constitute intelligent behaviour? If the criteria are too conservative, then the possibility of a being with intelligent behaviour quite unlike ours would be ruled out prematurely. But if the criteria are too liberal, then all sorts of movements will qualify as intelligent behaviour and we lose sight of what's special about the mind.

Epistemologically, this would be an improvement on substance dualism. Instead of having to work out whether something has an unobservable immaterial mind, we just have to observe whether it displays intelligent behaviour. And to discern what *kind* of mind it has, we just have to observe what kind of behaviour it displays. If I want to know whether the mind of an octopus is rational, whether it has emotions or whether it is conscious, I just have to observe the relevant behaviour. As above, though, there's a worry that behaviourism makes things *too* easy. If we managed to create an AI that behaved in all the ways a human does, there would still be a genuine question to ask about whether such a being has a mind and what kind of mind it has. Similarly, when we ask whether a plant, an insect or an amoeba has a mind, we are asking about *more* than how they behave. We want to know, for instance, whether these beings are *experiencing* anything on the inside. Yet the behaviourist dismisses such questions as unintelligible. Behaviourism's answer to the Distribution Question is thus too simplistic.

3.4 The Case for Identity Theory

Behaviourism did not enjoy a great deal of success. Even its progenitors didn't support the theory wholeheartedly. Hempel eventually rejected his theory due to the problem of circular definitions discussed above. And Ryle always stopped short of saying that mental terms could be given a behavioural analysis, once reporting that he was 'only one arm and one leg a behaviourist'. But behaviourism still had a dramatic impact in philosophy of mind, throwing down the gauntlet to other materialists to find a more credible theory of the mental. This gauntlet was picked up by the identity theorists. At the start of the chapter, I mentioned the growing science of brain and behaviour. Whereas behaviourists focused on the second of these, identity theorists focused on the first. They claimed that the mind is the same thing as the brain and that mental states are identical to brain states.

Identity theorists such as J. C. C. Smart (1920–2012) were inspired by the kinds of identity statement often found in scientific theories. Physics tells us that heat is mean kinetic energy and that lightning is an electrical discharge. Chemistry tells us that water is H_2O and that salt is NaCl. Biology tells us that chickenpox is *Varicella zoster* virus and that fits are epileptic seizures. These identity statements were arrived at by observing a perfect *correlation* between the two things that are identified, then explaining this correlation with the hypothesis that they are actually one and the same. The proposal is that the same kind of identity holds between mental states and brain states. Identity theorists often illustrate this with the example that pain is identical to C-fibres firing in the nervous system. This statement should not be read as ascribing a property to pain. Saying 'pain is C-fibres firing' is not like saying 'pain is unpleasant'. Rather, it is an identity statement asserting that pain and C-fibre firing are the very same thing, i.e. that pain = C-fibres firing. For Mindy to be in pain, for example, just is for Mindy's C-fibres to be firing.

Although C-fibres are a type of nerve fibre associated with pain, this standard example is quite unfortunate. For starters, there are clear cases of C-fibre activity without pain and of pain without C-fibre activity. More embarrassingly, C-fibres are found in the peripheral nervous system rather than the brain, so C-fibres firing is not even a brain state. That said, identity theorists aren't meant to be in the business of *discovering* identity statements. This is a job for neuroscientists. Just as chemists had to *discover* that water = H_2O, neuroscientists will have to discover that pain = brain state x, that a desire to score = brain-state-y and that perceiving green = brain-state-z. Although such mind–brain identity statements are not yet in our grasp, we can, the identity theorist argues, be confident that such identities obtain. And since brain states are material states, we can be confident that the mind is purely material. This route to materialism is quite different to that of the behaviourist. For behaviourists, the nature of a mental state can be determined a priori from the proverbial philosopher's armchair through a process of conceptual analysis. But for identity theorists, the nature of a mental state can only be discovered a posteriori through scientific inquiry.

We should be clear on what the meaning of these proposed identity statements is. It's important to distinguish between *types* and *tokens*. A type is a *kind* of thing – such as a specific brand of teapot – and a token is a specific *instance* of that type – such as the teapot on my shelf. Equipped with this distinction, we can differentiate between two different kinds of identity. There are two senses in which my teapot and your teapot might be identical. We might each have a teapot of the same kind, in which case our teapots would be *type-identical*. On the other hand, we might share the very same individual teapot, in which case my teapot and your teapot would be *token-identical*. Of course, if we share the same token teapot, then it can't be that your teapot is of a different type to mine, so things being token-identical *entails* that they are type-identical. But the entailment does not run the other way around – things can be type-identical without being the same token of that type.

The scientific statements we're considering are type-identity statements. Salt is a type exemplified by many tokens and NaCl is also a type exemplified by many tokens. The claim that salt = NaCl is the claim that these two types are identical – that being salt and being NaCl are the very same property. There are also mental state types exemplified by different tokens and brain state types exemplified by different tokens. Mental state types can be more or less coarse-grained. 'Desire-for-tea' is a fine-grained category of mental state, 'desire' is a more coarse-grained category and 'mental state' is a very coarse-grained category. Brain states can also be typed in more or less coarse-grained ways. Identity theory says that each mental state type is identical to a brain state type, so the property of being a pain state is identical to the property of being a brain state of type-x.

Identity theory is a bold position to take. If two things are identical, they must have all the same properties. After all, if one of them has a property that the other lacks, then they aren't really the same thing. If Spiderman really is Peter Parker, then any property of Spiderman is a property of Peter Parker, and vice versa. This means that if we can find just one property that things don't have in common, we can prove that they are not identical. If Peter Parker had toast for breakfast but Spiderman did not, then it must be false that Spiderman is Peter Parker. Similarly, if there is any property not shared both by my mental state and my brain state, then identity theory is false.

At first sight, it might seem like such counter-examples are easy to find. Pain states have the property of being disliked by Mindy but brain-state-x is not disliked by Mindy, therefore pain is not identical with brain-state-x. But the identity theorist has a simple rebuttal to cases like this. The brain state has exactly the same properties as the mental state, but Mindy just doesn't *realize* that the thing she dislikes is brain-state-x. This matches what we find with the ordinary identity statements made in science. I couldn't refute a chemist's claim that salt is NaCl by saying that I like salt but don't like NaCl. On the contrary, the fact that salt *is* NaCl entails that I do like NaCl after all.

A different line of attack on identity theory is to search for a property that brain states have but that mental states lack. Take the claim that the desire to score is brain-state-y. Mindy's brain-state-y has the property of being in a certain location. But Mindy's desire to score does not have the property of being located at all. Like all of Mindy's mental states, her desire to score has *no* location. The identity theorist can respond to this in much the same way. What the identification of mental states with brain states tells us is that, contra Descartes, mental states *do* have locations. Mindy might not be aware of her desires as having a location, but a surprising consequence of scientific inquiry is that her desire is in fact located somewhere in her head. Identity statements having such surprising consequences is not unprecedented. The claim that water is made of two gases certainly clashes with our everyday assumptions about water, but here common sense ought to give way to chemistry. Similarly, if neuroscience reveals that desires have a location, then our assumption that mental states are unlocated ought to be overturned.

Another way of challenging identity theory is to consider the 'phenomenal properties' of our experiences. These are the qualities that characterize how the experiences we undergo feel to us (and we'll be considering these further in chapter 5). When Mindy looks over the football pitch, her visual experience has a *greenish* quality (among various other qualities). Yet brain-state-z has no such greenish quality. So we ought to conclude that Mindy's perceptual experience is not identical to brain-state-z. In cases like this, it is hard for the identity theorist to insist that our brain states *do* in fact have such qualities. It looks pretty clear that there is nothing greenish in Mindy's head! However, the identity theorist U. T. Place (1924–2000) argues that objections of this ilk reflect a confusion about the nature of the qualities we perceptually experience. When Mindy looks around the pitch, she experiences a greenish quality. But it would be a mistake to attribute this quality *to her experience*. If anything is greenish, it is the football pitch and not Mindy's mental state.

Place's argument exploits the intentionality of the mental. As we saw in chapter 1, Mindy's perceptual experience is an intentional state – it is an experience *of* or *about* something. Just as a sentence in a book can be *about* something green without itself being green, so too Mindy's perceptual experience can be *about* the greenish quality of the pitch without itself having that property. To confuse properties of the things we experience with properties of the experience itself is to commit what Place calls the 'phenomenological fallacy', which he characterizes as 'the mistake of supposing that when the subject describes his experience, when he describes how things look, sound, smell, taste, or feel to him, he is describing the literal properties of objects and events on a peculiar sort of internal cinema or television screen' (1956: 49).

Once we free ourselves of this mistake, the alleged counter-example to identity theory dissolves away. Overall, identity theory has the tools to fend off these initial attacks.

3.5 Identity Theory and the Three Big Questions

3.5.1 *The Mind and Matter Question*

Identity theory claims that the relationship between mental states and material states is one of identity. Mindy's thoughts and emotions are no less material than her temperature or her height, and there is no need to posit immaterial entities to make sense of the mind. This proposal overcomes the issues around the causal closure of the physical that plagued substance dualism. According to causal closure, every physical event has a complete physical cause. Mindy kicking the ball is a physical event caused by contractions of her muscles, which are in turn caused by physical states of her brain, which are themselves caused by physical events in her environment. How does Mindy's intention to kick the ball fit into this story? According to identity theory, Mindy's intention *is* one of those physical brain states. So rather than having to intervene in the causally closed system of physical events from the outside, mental events are actually *parts* of that system.

The success of identity theory depends on the plausibility of mind–brain identity statements. So far, we've focused on the potential similarities between mind–brain identity statements and the established identity statements of science. But identity theory runs into difficulties when we start to reflect on the *differences* between these identity statements. In everyday life we're familiar with certain properties of salt: the way it dissolves in water, the way it stops ice forming on the doorstep and the way it preserves food. An important feature of the identity statement 'salt is NaCl' is that it is able to *explain* these properties. Once you understand what NaCl is, you can understand *why* salt dissolves in water, *why* it stops ice forming and *why* it preserves food. In fact, once you understand what NaCl is, you can work out that it is *inevitable* that salt has these properties. Given its chemical constitution, salt *couldn't but* dissolve in water and so on.

But with mind–brain identity statements, things are quite different. Joe Levine suggests that 'there seems to be nothing about C-fibre firing that makes it naturally "fit" the ... properties of pain' (1983: 356). And the same holds if 'C-fibres firing' is replaced with any brain state. A brain state will never explain why pain feels the way it does. No matter how much we know about a brain state, it seems possible that someone could be in that state without having a painful feeling at all. Something similar goes for any other proposed mind–brain identity statement. Why would this brain state constitute a perceptual experience of green, that brain state constitute a desire for tea and another brain state constitute an intention to kick? Levine calls this 'the explanatory gap'. This kind of worry about the relationship between brain and mind has a long history. For example, T. H. Huxley (1825–1895) offers this vivid assessment of the situation: 'How it is that anything so remarkable as a state of consciousness comes about as a result of irritating nervous tissue, is just as unaccountable as the appearance of Djin when Aladdin rubbed his lamp' (1866: 210).

The analogy with scientific identity statements is thus misleading. If brain states cannot *explain* the properties of our mental states, then mind–brain identity statements cannot be justified. A number of different responses to the explanatory gap have been offered. One is to deny that identity statements need have anything to do with explanation. On this view, pain *just is* brain-state-x and we shouldn't be expecting it to explain the properties of pain. Another option is to accept that identity statements must be explanatory but to deny that mind–brain identity statements fail this test. After all, neuroscience is a relatively young discipline and we don't yet have the relevant identity statements. Perhaps once we have them, we'll find that they do indeed explain the properties of our mental states. This is an important issue to which we'll return in the following chapters.

3.5.2 The Knowledge Question

According to identity theory, when we know that someone is in pain, the thing we know about is brain-state-x. Crucially, though, this doesn't entail that knowing someone is in pain requires knowing that they are in brain-state-x. To see why, consider what we find with other cases of identity. Although salt = NaCl, you can know that there is salt on the table without knowing that there is NaCl on the table. Nevertheless, if you know there's salt on the table, the thing you know about is NaCl, whether you realize it or not. Similarly, when we have knowledge of other minds, the things we know about are brain states, whether we realize it or not.

So how could we acquire such knowledge of other people's brains? Well, a person's brain states are manifest in their behaviour. Brain-state-x is a physical state that tends to cause wincing and crying out, so when I observe someone behaving in this way I can *infer* that they are in pain. Brain states also have typical causes. Twisting one's ankle tends to cause brain-state-x, so if I observe someone twisting their ankle I can again infer that they are in pain. Furthermore, identity theory allows for the possibility of observing someone's mental state *directly*. If a brain scan reveals that someone is in brain-state-x, you can know that they are in pain without having to observe anything about their behaviour or the recent history of their ankle.

Identity theory seems to account for our knowledge of other minds better than substance dualism or behaviourism. Substance dualism makes knowledge of other minds too hard, especially if it denies that behaviour is caused by mental states. Identity theory, in contrast,

can maintain that behaviour is indeed the causal manifestation of a person's mental states. That said, there
remains a worry about how we draw inferences about
the mental states of others. I might know what's going
on in *my* head when I wince and cry out, but am I really
justified in extrapolating that the same thing is going
on in your head when you behave that way? Perhaps
the worries about analogical reasoning raised against
substance dualism still have some bite against identity
theory.

Behaviourism made knowledge of other minds too
easy and failed to acknowledge the possibility of people
having mental states that don't match up with their
behaviour. But, for identity theory, behaviour is just an
indicator of someone's brain states, leaving open the
possibility of someone behaving in a certain way whilst
lacking the brain state/mental state that typically causes
that behaviour. So when we observe McDiver's pain
behaviour, it is an open possibility that she is not really
in brain-state-x at all and, as such, not really in pain.
By the same token, someone could be in a given brain
state without this being manifest in their behaviour. So
although the super-spartan's behaviour *suggests* that
they are not in pain, it is an open possibility that they
are in brain-state-x and therefore in pain.

Identity theory also promises to accommodate the
epistemic asymmetry of the mental. Mindy and the
team's medic can both know that Mindy is in pain. The
thing they both know about is Mindy's brain-state-x, but
the *way* that they know about it is very different. The
medic knows about it through observing its causes and
effects and maybe even by observing it on a brain scan.
But Mindy knows it *from the inside*. Her belief that she
is in pain might even be caused directly by brain-state-x.
This improves on behaviourism by accommodating the
fact that Mindy can know about her own pain *without
observation*. And it does this without going down the
dualist route of making the mind a private realm outside

the material world. The thing that Mindy knows about is a material state, but it is a material state that she can access in a way that others cannot.

3.5.3 The Distribution Question

Identity theory claims that all mental states are brain states, so a being has mental states if and only if it has the right brain states. This isn't quite the same as saying that having a mind is the same thing as having a brain – a dead body has a brain without having the specific *states* of the brain required for mentality. But even with this proviso, identity theory's answer to the Distribution Question is extremely brain-oriented. Can apes, cats or bees have beliefs, emotions or pains? Metaphysically, this is a simple matter of whether they have the relevant brain states – the very same brain states as constitute *our* beliefs, emotions and pains. And, epistemologically, knowing whether these creatures have those mental states is just a case of knowing about these brain states. Establishing that a cat has the anger brain state sounds like a major scientific undertaking. It would not, however, represent any special philosophical puzzle.

The problem for identity theory is that it is too *conservative*. Imagine discovering Martians with brains completely different to our own. Where our brains work by sending electrochemical signals, the Martian brain works through a complex system of hydraulics. Martians therefore share *no* brain states with humans. But if identity theory is true, that would entail they share no *mental* states with us. They can't have the same desires, the same emotions, the same perceptual experiences. Even if they showed all the outward signs of being in pain, the fact that Martians cannot be in brain-state-x entails that they cannot be in pain.

Identity theory's implausible answer to this hypothetical scenario is already problematic, but the problem becomes more acute when we consider some real-life cases. The nervous system of an octopus is dramatically different to that of a human. Octopuses do not, for example, have the C-fibres discussed earlier. It is at least an open possibility that an octopus feels pain, yet identity theory says that their neuroanatomy rules this out. The hardware of an artificial mind is even less like a human brain. It is at least an open possibility that an AI could have beliefs and memories, but states of a silicon chip are not brain states, so identity theory again rules this possibility out.

The objection here is not that Martians, octopuses and computers *do* have some of the same mental states as us. It might well transpire that they don't. The objection is that we shouldn't *rule out* the possibility of their having these mental states on the grounds that they lack brains like ours. The accusation is thus that identity theory offers too *anthropocentric* a view of the mind. It starts with an observation about how *our* mental states are constituted by brain states, then makes the wild leap to thinking that this is the *only* way that something could have those mental states.

There is a way of softening identity theory that promises to address this objection. We've been looking at *type* identity theory – the view that every mental state type is identical to a brain state type. This entails that the only way that something can be in pain – i.e. have a token mental state of the painful kind – is to be in brain-state-x. *Token* identity theory makes the more moderate claim that every instance of pain is token-identical to a material state and denies that there is a single material type shared by all tokens of pain. On this view, Mindy's token of pain is identical to Mindy's token of brain-state-x, and my token of pain is identical to my token of brain-state-x. The token pains of other creatures must be identical to *some* material state, but that state needn't be a token of brain-state-x. For Martians, their pain might be identical to some state of their hydraulic brain.

For the octopus or the computer, their pains would be identical to physical states of completely different types. According to token identity theory, mental kinds are *multiply realizable*. This means that the same type of mental state can be 'realized' in different physical states in different cases. Crucially, this is still a materialist theory. Every instance of pain is identical to *some* material state but *what kind* of material state that is can differ from case to case.

This proposal avoids the anthropocentrism of type identity theory. However, it faces a serious difficulty of its own. If a type of mental state is multiply realizable, we can ask what *unifies* all of its different realizations. What, for example, do these different material states of a human, a Martian and an octopus have in common that makes them all pains? It's tempting to answer that what they have in common is *their painfulness*. But what, on such a theory, is painfulness? It cannot be a *material* property shared by all these different states as they are completely different in their material nature. But if it's some *immaterial* property that accompanies these various material states, then it's no longer true that pains are identical to material states. Type identity theory didn't face this problem. On that version of the theory, the property that all pains have in common is the material property of all being brain states of type-x. So by softening this commitment of the identity theory, we have ended up leaving something important unexplained. If it *could* be explained, token identity theory might be revived. In chapter 4, we'll consider an attempt to do just that. As things stand, though, identity theory has significant limitations.

Key Concepts

Behaviourism: the theory that mental states are nothing more than patterns of actual and potential behaviour.

Identity theory: the theory that every mental state is identical to a physical state of the brain.

Multiple realizability: a mental state type is multiply realizable if different examples of that mental state can have different underlying constitutions.

Phenomenological fallacy: Place's name for confusing the properties we have experiences of for properties of the experience itself.

Token identity theory: the theory that every individual instance of a mental state is identical to some brain state, but that these brain states needn't be of the same physical kind.

Type identity theory: the theory that every type of mental state is identical to a type of brain state, meaning that two beings exemplifying the same kind of mental state must exemplify the same kind of physical state.

References and Further Reading

- Carl Hempel (1935), 'The Logical Analysis of Psychology', *Revue De Synthese* 10: 27–42. Excerpt reprinted in David J. Chalmers (ed.) (2021), *Philosophy of Mind: Classical and Contemporary Readings*, 2nd edn, New York: Oxford University Press. A classic formulation of behaviourism. Notice the emphasis Hempel places on the language we use to describe mental states.
- Gilbert Ryle (1949), *The Concept of Mind*, London: Hutchinson. Excerpt reprinted in Chalmers, *Philosophy of Mind*, op. cit. Here Ryle argues we are prone to a 'category mistake' in our thinking about the mind and makes his case against 'the dogma of the ghost in the machine'.
- Hilary Putnam (1968), 'Brains and Behaviour', *Analytical Philosophy* 11: 24–36. Excerpt reprinted in Chalmers, *Philosophy of Mind*, op. cit. Putnam

introduces his 'super-spartan' counter-example to behaviourism.

- J. J. C. Smart (1959), 'Sensations and Brain Processes', *Philosophical Review* 68: 141–56. Reprinted in Chalmers, *Philosophy of Mind*, op. cit. In this paper, Smart makes his influential case for type identity theory, drawing careful analogies with scientific identity statements.

- U. T. Place (1956), 'Is Consciousness a Brain Process?', *British Journal of Psychology* 47: 44–50. Reprinted in Chalmers, *Philosophy of Mind*, op. cit. Here Place argues that resistance to identity theory is based on the 'phenomenological fallacy'.

- Joseph Levine (1983), 'Materialism and Qualia: The Explanatory Gap', *Pacific Philosophical Quarterly* 64: 354–61. Reprinted in Chalmers, *Philosophy of Mind*, op. cit. Levine presents a problem for identity theory, arguing that there's an 'explanatory gap' between physical states and some kinds of mental state.

- T. H. Huxley (1866), *Lessons in Elementary Physiology*, London: Macmillan. Lesson VIII contains the classic formulation, quoted above, of the problem faced by materialists. But this isn't really a text to be grappled with.

4

Functionalism and the Computer Revolution

4.1 Functionalism in Context

Functionalism is a theory built on the idea that the mind is like a computer. Perhaps unsurprisingly, the emergence of this view is bound up with the emergence of the discipline of artificial intelligence. In the 1950s, researchers started to take seriously the idea that the intelligent processes performed by a human mind could be matched, and even improved upon, by machines. Before this time, the notion of a thinking machine had been widely dismissed. As we saw in chapter 2, Descartes was arguing in the seventeenth century that thinking machines were impossible. So what changed in the intervening years to make researchers think that such machines were not only possible but buildable within a generation? The key changes occurred at both the level of theory and the level of engineering.

At the level of theory, new conceptual tools were developed for thinking about how computational processes could work. The philosopher and mathematician Alan Turing (1912–1954) offered a conceptual framework for understanding how a computer could be programmed to perform any kind of computation. This framework built on developments in the formalization of mathematics, pioneered by philosophers such as Gottlob Frege (1848–1925), Bertrand Russell (1872–1970) and Alfred North Whitehead (1861–1947). These theoretical insights explained how, in principle, a machine could perform complex calculations. But putting these principles into practice would require huge steps forward in computer engineering.

In the early nineteenth century, the mathematician Charles Babbage (1791–1871) drew up plans for his Analytical Engine. Widely regarded as the first computer, this steam-driven machine was designed to produce number tables by receiving instructions through punch cards, then computing the results through an elaborate system of gears. Although Babbage was concerned with the computation of numbers, his collaborator Ada Lovelace (1815–1852) realized that the machine might be used to compute *any* symbol that it could be programmed to process:

> [The Analytical Engine] might act upon other things besides number, were objects found whose mutual fundamental relations could be expressed by those of the abstract science of operations, and which should be also susceptible of adaptations to the action of the operating notation and mechanism of the engine ... Supposing, for instance, that the fundamental relations of pitched sounds in the science of harmony and of musical composition were susceptible of such expression and adaptations, the engine might compose elaborate and scientific pieces of music of any degree of complexity or extent. (Lovelace 1843: 694, Note A)

Sadly, the designs for this vast machine were so ambitious that Babbage never managed to build it. But later engineers would succeed where Babbage failed, first building mechanical machines similar to the Analytical Engine then upgrading to electromechanical machines such as the World War II code-breaking machine on which Alan Turing famously worked. In the 1950s, the size, cost and reliability of computers were dramatically improved by the development of the silicon transistors we use today. And by then, computers were already performing feats far beyond what Descartes could have conceived, like solving complex word problems, proving mathematical theorems and beating humans at draughts.

The development of these *artificial* minds inspired important new ideas about our own *biological* minds. Most importantly, it encouraged the idea that the mind itself is a kind of computer. Computers are, in essence, information processors. They take *inputs* from the world, they *process* that input in a certain way, then produce *outputs*. For Babbage's machine, the inputs were punch cards and the outputs were number tables. For Alexa, the inputs are voice commands and the outputs are audio streams. Although these machines work in very different ways, the thing that makes them both computers is that they process information. The mind can be understood as doing just the same thing. Mindy's mind receives sensory inputs from the world around her, it processes those inputs in a certain way, then it produces the output of bodily actions. On this view, the human mind is a biological computer.

Regarding the mind as a biological computer opens up a new way of framing the relationship between the mind and the brain. If you want to understand how a smartphone works, you can investigate it at two different levels. At the level of *software*, you can establish how the phone is programmed. And at the level of *hardware*, you can determine how the physical components of the phone run that software. Something similar goes for how the mind works. We can explore the 'software' of the mind, i.e. the structure of our mental processes. Or we can explore the 'hardware' of the mind, i.e. the soggy grey matter on which this software runs. Cognitive psychologists can determine how information is processed in the mind whilst bracketing questions about how these processes are 'realized' in the brain. And neuroscientists can determine how neural processes work whilst bracketing questions about what kinds of information our neurons are processing. In practice, of course, it is important in both computing and psychology to understand how the hardware and software fit together. But the very distinction between these two levels of investigation is extremely useful.

One useful application is to the *multiple realizability* of mental states. One of the most significant problems for type identity theory was that different beings can plausibly share the same type of mental state without sharing the same type of physical state. But, once we see mental states as being like states of a computer, an elegant solution presents itself. The same software can be installed on completely different hardware – a programme for dividing numbers, for instance, could be run on the silicon chip of your mobile phone or on the cogs and gears of Babbage's Analytical Engine. Software is thus *multiply realizable* in different kinds of physical hardware. So if the mind is like the software of the brain, then the same mental states could be realized in different kinds of physical brain. A human, an octopus and a Martian could have completely different biological hardware, but this needn't preclude them from having the same mental states. Perhaps these mental states could even be realized in the hardware of a computer. We'll unpack these ideas properly later on but their initial appeal should be clear.

The mind–computer analogy has its roots in some much older philosophical ideas. The analogy with computers is premised on the idea that mental states should be characterized in terms of what they *do* rather than in terms of their internal constitution. This general approach was taken by Aristotle (384–322 BCE) and later by Hobbes (1588–1679). Though they didn't frame it in terms of computation, they argued that the mind should be understood in terms of its activities rather than in terms of what it is made of. The mind–computer analogy says the same thing, adding that the activities in question are activities of information processing.

Although promising, the mind–computer analogy itself doesn't provide us with a theory of the mental. What we need is a theory that builds on the mind–computer analogy to offer an account of what mental states are and what distinguishes the different types of mental state from each other. Functionalism is designed to do just this.

4.2 The Case for Functionalism

Functionalism was developed by philosophers such as D. M. Armstrong (1926–2014). It claims that the different types of mental state – beliefs, desires, memories, etc. – are distinguished by the different functions that they perform. The mind is made up of a whole economy of mental states that perform different roles and that interact with each other in different ways. Memories, for instance, play a distinctive role in our mental economy that is quite different to the role played by desires. Functionalists argue that what *makes* a mental state a memory is that it performs the functional role distinctive to memories.

To make sense of this claim, we should step back from mental states for a moment and think about other things that are defined by their functional role. Consider what it means for an organ to be a heart. Something is a heart in virtue of performing the role of pumping blood around the body. Although the human heart has a particular physical constitution, this is not what makes it a heart. If a creature has a blood-pumping organ with a different physical constitution, it would still qualify as a heart because of the function it performs. Put another way, hearts are multiply realizable. Conversely, if a quirk of evolution produced creatures with organs exactly like human hearts in their physical constitution but that served the function of pumping waste rather than blood, then those organs would not qualify as hearts.

Being a heart is thus a property that an organ has in virtue of the role it plays in a specific system viz. the organism. If we turn our attention to other kinds of system, we can find other functional properties. A car is a mechanical system made of various parts. In a car, the carburettor has the function of mixing oxygen and fuel for combustion. As with the heart, something is a carburettor in virtue of performing this role and not in virtue of the particular physical constitution it happens to have. A game of football is also a kind of system with various roles defined by the rules of the game. In a football game, someone is a team's goalkeeper in virtue of the distinctive role they play in the game – a role quite different to that of the outfield players or the referee. When a team's goalkeeper is substituted, they cease to play that role and so cease to be the goalkeeper. And the substitute becomes the goalkeeper by taking on that role in their place.

Reflecting on different kinds of system takes us back to computers. A computer is an information-processing system in which different parts or states of the system perform different roles. A computer state is a memory, for example, in virtue of the functional role that it plays – the role of storing information for later use. That's why, as discussed at the start of the chapter, computational states are multiply realizable. It doesn't matter whether that role is performed by a structure in a silicon chip or by a configuration of cogs and gears; as long as it performs that role, then it qualifies as a memory.

So how does all of this apply to mental states? Functionalists propose that a mental state is the kind of mental state it is in virtue of the functional role that it plays in the mind. In order to specify what pain is, for example, you must specify what pain *does*. Pain occurs in response to particular kinds of sensory input – specifically, the kinds associated with bodily damage. Pain causes other mental states, such as a desire to avoid the source of the pain. And pain generates behavioural outputs, such as crying out. This is just a very simple sketch of the function of pain. The full story would involve a much more detailed account of its functional role, and there is some debate among functionalists about how we should approach fleshing out this role. We'll explore this in more detail at the end of the chapter, but the key point is that there is a 'pain role' that pains perform. According to functionalism, a token mental state is a pain in virtue of playing this role. So Mindy is in pain because she has a mental state that is playing the pain role. Visual states perform a different role – they are caused by sensory inputs, produce beliefs about the immediate environment, and so on. A mental state is a visual state if and only if it plays this role. Desires perform yet another role – they are caused by the organism's needs, they cause behaviour that will meet those needs, and so on. A mental state is a desire if and only if it plays this role.

One thing to note is that you cannot specify what a mental state does without mentioning *other* mental states. Whether a pain causes you to cry out depends on your other mental states. Mindy has a pain in her ankle but, because of everything else going on in her mind, does not show any pain behaviour. A desire for tea only causes Bob to open a tea caddy *if* he has the belief that the tea caddy contains tea. Conversely, a belief that there's tea in the caddy only causes Bob to open it *if* he desires tea. There's thus a kind of *circularity* inherent in the specification of functional roles. This circularity is to be expected. If you want to specify the role distinctive to a goalkeeper, you'd have to mention outfield players, the referee and so on. And if you wanted to specify the roles of outfield players and the referee, you'd have to mention the goalkeeper. The same goes for the role of organs in the body or parts in a car or programmes on a computer. Each of the different functional roles in a system is *interdefinable*.

In chapter 3, we saw that a major objection to behaviourism is that its analyses of mental terms were circular. Why, then, is it okay for functionalists to have circular definitions? The difference is this. Behaviourists claim that any sentence involving mental terms can be *translated* into a sentence about behaviour that has no mental terms. But if the behaviour definitive of a mental state can only be specified with reference to other mental states, then this project is doomed to fail. Functionalism has no such ambition. It allows that the functional role of a mental state can only be specified with reference to other mental states. Functionalism never promised to *translate away* mental terms, so there's nothing wrong with including mental terms in the characterization of functional roles. The fact that mental terms are *interdefinable* only becomes a problem if you're trying to translate descriptions of the mental into descriptions of the non-mental. But this would be like trying to define what a goalkeeper is without mentioning any of the other roles in a football game: it can't be done and, more importantly, there's no need to do it! We're quite capable of understanding the different roles played in a football game without them being translated into terms that make no reference to those roles.

How does intentionality fit into the picture? We have already seen that many mental states – perhaps *all* mental states – have intentionality. Mindy's perceptual experience is about the football, her desire to score is about her scoring and her elation is about her team's victory. Another way of putting this is that these mental states *represent* the world in certain ways. Mindy's perception represents something in her environment, her desire represents what she aims to do and her emotion represents the value of her success. Many have attempted to explain the intentionality of mental states using a functionalist framework. The idea is that a state is a representation when it has the *function* of representing something. Mindy's perceptual state, for example, has the function of representing the presence of the ball. Mindy's state has the ball as its intentional object precisely because it performs this ball-representing function. Crucially, this explains how it's possible for our mental states to *mis*represent things. If Mindy hallucinates a football, then she is in a perceptual state that is *meant* to occur when she's looking at a football but that has mistakenly occurred when no such football is present. Taking this line of thought further, if intentionality is the mark of the mental, then we can regard the mind as a system of intentional states, each with its own representational function. These applications of functionalism are optional, so I'll put them aside during our evaluation of the theory. Nevertheless, the fact that functionalism could help explain the intentionality of mental states might be regarded as a point in its favour.

Now that we've pinned down the functionalist proposal, we can ask what motivates such a view. The most powerful reason for adopting functionalism is that it seems to capture what's important about mental states. Regardless of one's stance on functionalism, it seems that each type of mental state is associated with a functional role. Desires do one thing and beliefs another. And, at the more fine-grained level, desires-for-tea do one thing and desires-to-score do another. Functionalism says that performing the functional role associated with a mental state type-M is *sufficient* for being a mental state of type-M. So to resist functionalism, one would have to specify what *extra* thing is needed for something to be a mental state M. What properties, besides doing what M-states do, must a state have to qualify as an M-state? If a critic cannot offer a plausible response, the functionalist can claim victory. Let's call this the *What-More-Do-You-Want? Argument*.

Consider   how   the   What-More-Do-You-Want?

Argument plays out for memories. If a state is performing the function of retaining information for later use, what more could you possibly require for it to qualify as a memory? And if a state is doing everything that desires do – such as guiding the creature's behaviour towards the fulfilment of a goal – how could one doubt that it constitutes a desire? And if a state is doing everything that beliefs do – such as being used in rational inferences – why would anything else be needed for it to count as a belief?

A comparison with other functional properties helps capture the force of this argument. If an organ is doing what a heart does, what else could possibly be needed for it to qualify as a heart? You might say that a heart has to have a particular physical constitution with particular cells in a particular structure, but we've already seen that features of the heart-role's *realizer* should not be confused with the nature of the heart itself. A heart is what it does, so anyone throwing non-functional criteria into the mix has just misunderstood what it means to be a heart. The same is true for carburettors, goalkeepers and computer software. And the functionalist can say exactly the same thing about mental states. If a state is doing what a memory, desire or belief does, then it is thereby a memory, desire or belief. To ask for anything more is to misunderstand what kind of thing memories, desires and beliefs are. Borrowing Ryle's phrase, we might even say that such a critic is guilty of a *category mistake* about the nature of the mental.

Although this argument gets functionalism a long way, there are some mental states that do not lend themselves so readily to a functionalist analysis. Consider pain again. If an octopus is in a state that does everything a pain does – such as being caused by bodily damage and causing the creature to recoil – what more could we require for it to qualify as a pain? Well, we could require that it *feels* the way that pain feels. We all know what pain feels like and it's reasonable to suggest that if things don't feel that way for the octopus, then it's not really in pain. Of course, it's in a mental state that has the same *outward manifestations* as pain. But if it doesn't feel like pain *on the inside*, then that state shouldn't qualify as a pain. What a mental state *does* is one thing, but how a mental state *feels* is another. So to the extent that a mental state type is distinguished by what it feels like to be in that mental state, it will be resistant to a purely functional explanation.

It's pretty clear that a mental state only qualifies as a pain if it feels a certain way for the subject who has that mental state. Other cases are less clear-cut. Is being in a state that does the things that anger does sufficient for being angry? Or does being angry also require you to *feel* a particular way? Is being in a state that does the things that a taste of bitterness does sufficient for tasting bitterness? Or does tasting bitterness involve having a distinctive kind of experience? Is being in a state that does the things that imagining a dragon does suffice for imagining a dragon? Or does imagining a dragon require one to undergo a particular type of experience?

When the What-More-Do-You-Want? Argument works, it works very well and highlights the appeal of functionalism. But when it doesn't work, it highlights a potentially serious gap in the functionalist theory. That gap is the *subjective* side of the mind: what our mental states feel like from the inside; how our mental life seems from the first-person perspective; our conscious experiences. The challenge of explaining conscious experience has led many functionalists to put consciousness to one side. Adopting a *divide-and-conquer* strategy, they seek to explain everything about the mind apart from conscious experience, then try to deal with this explanatory residue separately. Exactly *how* to deal with this residue is a tricky and contentious topic that deserves a chapter of its own, so in chapter 5 I'll look at this in detail. In the meantime, though, we'll allow the functionalist to adopt this divide-and-conquer strategy and consider how well

it deals with the Three Big Questions if conscious experience is kept out of the picture.

4.3 Functionalism and the Three Big Questions

4.3.1 The Mind and Matter Question

Functionalism gives us an interesting picture of the
relationship between mind and matter. According to
functionalism, having a particular mental state means
having a state that plays a particular functional role.
Every mental state is defined by its functional role, and
the functional role of each mental state type can be specified without mentioning the brain. We can capture what
a desire is, for example, by mapping how a desire relates
to inputs, outputs and other mental states. A functional
role is an abstract structure, and an abstract structure
is not a physical thing. So functionalism doesn't sound
much like a materialist view of the mind.

However, functional roles have to be *realized* by
something. Mindy's desire to score is what it is because
of the functional role it plays, but that abstract role
must be performed by something concrete. This is where
physical states of the brain fit into the picture. The desire-
to-score role is played by a particular state of Mindy's
brain, such as brain-state-y. If we consider other kinds
of functional property, we find that they too are abstract
roles with physical realizers. The heart role is performed
by a physical organ, the carburettor role is performed by
a physical car part and the goalkeeper role is performed
by a physical person. Mindy's desire to score is thus
a functional state with a physical realizer. Immaterial
minds are not part of the picture, so functionalism is
starting to sound more like a materialist view.

So is functionalism a materialist theory or not? The
answer is that functionalism is *neutral* on whether
mental states are physical or non-physical. It says that

someone has a desire to score in virtue of having *some-thing* that performs the relevant functional role. But *what* performs that role is left completely open, meaning that functionalism is compatible with anti-materialist views like substance dualism. Imagine that Mindy has an immaterial mind and that this mind is in a state caused by inputs from her environment and that causes her to kick the ball. This immaterial state of Mindy's Cartesian mind plays the functional role of a desire-to-score so, according to functionalism, it *is* a desire to score. There's nothing about the nature of desire that requires desires to be physical or non-physical.

Does that mean functionalists don't take a stand on whether mental states are material or immaterial? Not quite. Although functionalism is *compatible* with dualism, almost all functionalists claim that our mental states are in fact realized by physical states of the brain. Mindy's desire *could* have been realized by a state of an immaterial soul, but in reality it's realized by some brain state such as brain-state-y. Materialist functionalism thus combines two theses:

1   All mental states are functional states
2   All actual realizers of mental states are physical states

This materialist functionalism seems to overcome the problems faced by identity theory. Type identity theory claimed that every mental state type is identical to a physical state type. For instance, the mental property of desiring to score is identical to the physical property of being in brain-state-y. A key problem with this view was the *multiple realizability* of mental states. A theory shouldn't preclude an octopus or a Martian from desiring to score just because they lack the same brain states as us (earlier I raised this point in terms of pain but we're putting pain experiences aside for current purposes). Functionalism accommodates the multiple realizability of desires by saying that a desire is a functional property and that this same functional role can be realized in different ways by different beings. In Mindy, the desiring-to-score role is realized by brain-state-y, but in an octopus or a Martian different kinds of physical state might perform that role. It might even be that this desire is realized by different brain states in different humans.

Materialist functionalism thus advocates a version of token identity theory. It says that every specific instance of desiring to score is identical to some specific physical state, whilst denying that these physical states must all be of the same physical type. We saw in chapter 3 that the problem for token identity theorists was that they couldn't explain what *unified* all these different physical states as being of the same mental type. It's all very well saying that the diverse states of Mindy, the octopus and the Martian are all desires to score, but what do these different physical states have in common that explains how they each constitute the same kind of mental state? Functionalism has the answer: each of these physical tokens performs the *same functional role*. So although these states are all of different *physical* types, they are each of the same *functional* type and, thereby, of the same *mental* type.

So why should a functionalist go down the materialist route rather than staying neutral on the question of materialism? One consideration is *parsimony*. When we're choosing between competing theories, we should generally prefer the least complex theory. Materialist functionalism says there's a world of material things, some of which are the realizers of mental states. Immaterialist functionalism says there's a world of material things *and that there are immaterial souls*. This makes it the less economical theory. Of course, there are times when we *need* to posit new things to explain a phenomenon. But when it comes to mental states, there is no such need. Physical states are perfectly capable of realizing mental states, so positing immaterial minds is unnecessary.

Another argument for materialist functionalism pertains to causation. We've already seen that dualism has trouble with mental causation, and these problems would persist for an immaterialist functionalism. If the realizers of our mental states were immaterial, then they wouldn't be able to cause anything. If Mindy's desire was realized by a state of her immaterial soul, then the causal closure of the physical would preclude it from causing her to kick the ball. But if Mindy's desire is realized by a state of her physical brain, this problem disappears. Her desire is realized by a physical state that falls *within* the causally closed system of the physical, so there is nothing to preclude this state from causing her actions.

Materialist functionalism thus promises to make sense of the causal efficacy of mental states in a way that immaterialist functionalism cannot. Doubts can be raised, however, about whether functionalism can make good on this promise. We've been distinguishing all along between a functionally defined mental state and the physical state that realizes it. But which of these two things causes someone's behaviour? Mindy's desire to score is realized by brain-state-y. But does Mindy kick the ball because of the kind of brain state she is in or because of the kind of functional role that state is playing? If she kicks the ball because of the kind of physical brain state she's in, then the functional role of that brain state is causally irrelevant. And if mental states are functional states, then this would amount to epiphenomenalism. But if she kicks the ball because of the functional role of that state, then it's not the physical features of her state that are doing the causal work, which raises worries about the causal closure of the physical.

This dilemma raises some deep and difficult questions about the metaphysics of causation. Defenders of functionalism respond by arguing that we don't have to choose between brain-based explanations and functional explanations. There is one causal process leading up to Mindy's kick, and that process can be described at the level of neurons firing or at the level of functional processes. For comparison, think about how Alexa's audio stream could be explained at the level of its programming or at the level of the physical hardware that realizes that programming. The point is that functionalism is a long way from interactionist dualism, which says there are actually two completely distinct causes behind Mindy's kick. So although there's no knockdown objection to functionalism here, it's worth noting that it might not be able to accommodate mental causation quite as easily as it seems.

4.3.2 The Knowledge Question

If functionalism is true, to be in a mental state of a particular type is to be in a state with a particular set of causes and effects. This suggests a straightforward account of how we gain knowledge of other minds. I might not be able to see your mental states, but what I *can* see are some of their causes and effects. And by seeing these causes and effects, I can determine what mental states you have. The functionalist's mind–computer analogy points us in the right direction here. How do I know that my computer has just run an antivirus scan? Well, I can't look inside my computer and see the microscopic processes occurring in its silicon chips (and even if I could, I wouldn't understand them!). But what I can see are the causes and effects of the antivirus scan. I know about the computer's *inputs*, like me clicking 'Scan' on the interface for the antivirus software. And I know about the computer's *outputs*, like the 'Scan Complete' notification that appeared on the screen and the computer's improved performance following the scan. From this I can infer that a particular process has occurred in the computer.

So how could we know that Mindy had the intention

to kick the ball? Well, we can see that she is in the kind of situation that *causes* intentions-to-kick. We know that people who are awarded a penalty tend to form that intention. Furthermore, we can see that she actually kicked the ball and we know that such behaviour is typically caused by an intention to kick. If we know the functional role distinctive of intentions-to-kick, and we know the relevant inputs and outputs of Mindy's mind, we are in a good position to know that she had the intention to kick. This model of our epistemic position is far preferable to that offered by substance dualists. For substance dualists, a person's behaviour cannot provide a window onto someone's mind because the connection between mental states and behaviour is completely contingent. According to epiphenomenal dualism, mental states don't even *cause* behaviour. Functionalism offers a very different account, claiming that the causes and effects of a mental state are what make it the kind of mental state it is.

When discussing behaviourism in chapter 3, we considered the worry that behaviourism made knowledge of other minds *too* easy. Can the same objection be levelled against functionalism? For the behaviourist, intending to kick the ball is *nothing more than* having certain behavioural dispositions. For the functionalist, though, intending to kick the ball means having a state that performs a certain functional role, and exactly how that state is manifested in our behaviour is left open. Our behaviour is the product of interactions between a host of functional states, and different combinations of functional state could explain the very same behaviour. The most likely possibility is that Mindy's behaviour was caused by her intention to kick the ball. But it's at least *possible* that the kick was instead caused by an intention to kick a cabbage combined with a belief that the object before her was a cabbage. In this case, it's pretty obvious what the right explanation is, but in many cases people's behaviour is ambiguous. Functionalism can accommodate such ambiguity in a way that behaviourism cannot: even if you've observed all of someone's behaviour, you might not know what internal functional process generated that behaviour and so might not know what mental states they have.

Overall then, functionalism carves out a plausible middle ground between substance dualism and behaviourism. Substance dualism offers an account of mental states that commits them to *underestimating* our ability to know about the minds of others. Behaviourism, in contrast, offers an account that *overestimates* our epistemological position. Functionalism seems to strike a perfect balance, explaining how we could know about the mental states of others whilst making sense of the doubts we might have about what's going on in someone else's mind.

Regarding knowledge of our own minds, functionalism again offers a plausible account. It accommodates the *epistemic asymmetry* of knowledge quite straightforwardly. We can only know about Mindy's mental states via their external causes and effects. But Mindy has an internal way of accessing her mental states that is unavailable to anyone else. The functional role of a mental state is not just to cause certain behaviours but to cause other mental states. Part of the functional role of an intention is to cause a belief that one has that intention, and part of the functional role of a desire is to cause a belief that one has that desire and so on. If Mindy's mental states reliably cause her to have accurate beliefs about those mental states, she can know what's going on in her own mind directly. This *first-person* access to one's mind is precisely what's missing from the behaviourist's account. Mindy doesn't need to observe her own behaviour to know about her own mental states because she can access those states internally.

4.3.3 *The Distribution Question*

Functionalism claims that a mind is a system of interacting mental states each defined by the functional role it plays. Although *our* mental states are realized by certain types of brain state, the mental states of other beings might be realized in completely different ways. If we want to know whether something has a particular kind of mental state, we just need to identify the functional role distinctive to that mental state, then see whether our candidate has a state that performs that functional role. So far we've been working with very simple sketches of the functional roles of each mental state, so we'd first need to pin down these functional roles in much more detail. But how exactly this should be done is a source of significant disagreement among functionalists.

One school of thought says that we can characterize each role using common sense. We already know what anger does, for example, because it is built into the meaning of the word 'anger'. We can thus specify the anger role a priori by analysing the meaning of 'anger'. This view is known as analytic functionalism. Another school of thought says that if we want to know the nature of anger, we need to look at anger itself, rather than just reflecting on the meaning of our words. On this view, a full account of the anger role must be based on a posteriori investigation. If psychology reveals that anger performs a function that goes beyond our common-sense conception of it, then we ought to build this into our specification of the anger role. This view is known as empirical functionalism, or psycho-functionalism.

When asked to specify the role essential to each mental state type, analytic and empirical functionalists will give different answers. Empirical functionalism builds a lot more detail into the functional role of each mental state type. The anger role, for example, includes obvious things as being caused by certain kinds of threatening situation and causing certain kinds of aggressive behaviour. But it might also include less obvious things like being caused by certain hormones, causing increased heart rate, enhancing attention to the anger-inducing situation and decreasing the tendency for rational evaluation. Analytic functionalism, on the other hand, does not include these extra criteria and so allows more things to qualify as anger states. So how should we choose between them? Put simply, we want a theory that is neither too liberal nor too conservative in its attribution of mental states.

Consider what each view would say about whether an octopus can be angry. When an octopus faces off against another octopus in its territory, it could easily be in a mental state that performs the role we associate with anger. It would, for instance, have a state caused by a threatening situation and that causes aggressive behaviour. So long as the state meets these common-sense criteria, the analytic functionalist would conclude that the octopus is angry. For the empirical functionalist, however, there are more specific criteria that the octopus might not meet. Perhaps the octopus's mental state is not caused by the relevant hormones (remember, the octopus has a very different physiology to us). And perhaps it does not decrease the octopus's tendency for rational evaluation (maybe the octopus doesn't even have a capacity for rational evaluation). Here empirical functionalists could reasonably be criticized for being too conservative. They're denying that the octopus is angry because its anger doesn't function in the very specific way that *our* anger functions. In this case, the more liberal approach taken by the analytic functionalists seems to yield the right answer.

But now consider another case. A self-driving car could have a state that performs the role we associate with anger. It could be caused by a threatening situation – such as another car pulling out in front of it – and cause 'aggressive' behaviour – such as beeping its horn and revving its engine. If this state of the car functions in the relevant way, analytic functionalists would have to say that the car is angry. Here it seems that the broad criteria used by the analytic functionalist might be *too* liberal. Empirical functionalists give a different answer. Although the car has a state that does *some* of the things associated with anger, it does *not* have a state that plays the full functional role of anger. The state is not caused by particular hormones, does not cause increased heart rate, does not influence the focus of attention or the tendency to rational evaluation. So here the more demanding criteria of the empirical functionalist seem to yield a better result.

This leaves us in something of a bind. Sometimes we want analytic functionalism's liberal criteria and sometimes we want the more stringent criteria of empirical functionalism. Rather than picking between them, perhaps the best strategy is to find a *balance* between these two approaches. Our a priori conception of a mental state's functional role must be supplemented with further criteria that are determined a posteriori, but *which* further criteria should make the cut would have to be worked out carefully to avoid anthropocentrism and to strike the balance between being too liberal and being too conservative.

As things stand then, functionalism doesn't provide clear answers to the Distribution Question. What it *does* do, however, is offer a framework for answering the question. First we specify the functional role of a mental state type, then we see whether a candidate has states that perform that role. Work is needed to get the functional criteria right, and then work is needed to determine whether our target has mental states that meet the criteria. But perhaps this is as much as we should expect from a theory of the mental. After all, it's implausible that the Distribution Question could be answered from the proverbial philosopher's armchair without the aid of a posteriori inquiry.

Key Concepts

Analytic functionalism: the view that the functional role definitive of a mental state type can be determined a priori from our common-sense conception of how that mental state functions.

Empirical functionalism/psycho-functionalism: the view that the functional role definitive of a mental state type must be determined a posteriori through scientific inquiry.

Functionalism: the theory that what makes something a particular type of mental state is the way it functions in a system and not its internal constitution.

Materialist functionalism: the theory that these functional roles are always realized by physical states. This view entails token identity theory but not type identity theory.

Mind–computer analogy: the view that the mind is (or is like) a computer in that it receives inputs of information and processes them to produce outputs.

References and Further Reading

- Alan Turing (1950), 'Computing Machinery and Intelligence', *Mind* 59: 433–60. Excerpt reprinted in David J. Chalmers (ed.) (2021), *Philosophy of Mind: Classical and Contemporary Readings*, 2nd edn, New York: Oxford University Press. The method of testing for intelligence that would become known as the 'Turing test' is introduced in this hugely influential paper.
- Ada Lovelace (1843), 'Notes on L. Menabrea's "Sketch of the Analytical Engine Invented by Charles Babbage, Esq."', *Taylor's Scientific Memoirs* 3. These notes contain the prescient remarks, quoted above, about the possibilities of artificial intelligence.

The rest of the notes aren't really relevant so this isn't a text to seek out.

- Hilary Putnam (1967), 'The Nature of Mental States', *Art, Mind, and Religion*: 37–48. Reprinted in Chalmers, *Philosophy of Mind*, op. cit. This early formulation of functionalism set the stage for much future work.
- David M. Armstrong (1981), 'The Causal Theory of the Mind', in *The Nature of Mind and Other Essays*, Ithaca: Cornell University Press. Reprinted in Chalmers, *Philosophy of Mind*, op. cit. Here Armstrong makes a case in favour of functionalism.

5

The Problem of Consciousness

5.1 Inconvenient Truths

In the last chapter we saw that functionalism – or, more specifically, materialist functionalism – offers a promising theory with substantial advantages over its competitors. But we let functionalists get away with putting aside an aspect of the mind that they found inconvenient: conscious experience. It seems that functionalism cannot explain what our mental states feel like on the inside. Having a state that plays the functional role of pain is one thing, but *experiencing* pain is quite another. Functionalism tells us what a pain state *does* but not what it is like to *be* in that pain state for the subject. The other materialist theories we've discussed faced much the same problem. Behaviourists could not explain our conscious experiences in terms of patterns of behaviour. Feeling pain, for example, is not just a matter of having certain behavioural dispositions. And type identity theorists could not explain our conscious experiences in terms of our having a certain neural state. There is an 'explanatory gap' between facts about what's happening in your brain and facts about your pain experience. This problem for materialism is serious enough to deserve a name: the Problem of Consciousness. The Problem of Consciousness is the problem of explaining conscious experience in terms of physical states and/or functional states ('physico-functional' states for short).

At this stage, it's worth refining our terminology a little. Following Ned Block, we can distinguish between *phenomenal* consciousness and *access* consciousness. A mental state is *phenomenally conscious* if and only if there's something it's like to be in that state for the subject that has it. This term is derived from the Greek word *phenomenon*, which means *appearing to view*. The idea is that your phenomenal consciousness constitutes how things appear to you. When we say that someone's mental state is conscious, we often mean that it is *phenomenally* conscious, i.e. that the subject *experiences* this mental state.

But there is another sense of the word 'conscious' that is not directly concerned with experience. A mental state might be conscious in the sense of being available for a subject's wider mental processes, such as its use in a chain of reasoning or the guidance of voluntary behaviour. Imagine that Mindy sees the big screen at the game briefly flash an advert for Jaffa Cakes. We can ask whether Mindy saw the advert consciously or unconsciously. If Mindy's perceptual state is conscious, she could use her perception of the advert to guide her reasoning, e.g. she might make the inference that Jaffa Cakes are sponsoring the game. She could also use her perception to guide her actions, e.g. if asked, she would report that she saw the advert. But if her perception of the advert was unconscious, then it wouldn't be available to her in these ways. If asked, she wouldn't report that she'd seen the advert, nor would she use this unconscious perception to guide her reasoning and action. Block calls this kind of consciousness *access* consciousness.

A state being access conscious is not equivalent to it being phenomenally conscious. If we knew that an octopus had mental states that were accessible to guide its actions, we would still face the further question of whether the octopus was experiencing anything on the inside. That's because a state could be access conscious without being phenomenally conscious. Access consciousness is a functional notion describing how a mental state fits into the wider economy of the mind. So to explain access consciousness, all you have to do is pin down this functional role and the brain states that realize it. Phenomenal consciousness, on the other hand, is uniquely resistant to physico-functional explanation. Chalmers (1997) contrasts the 'easy problem' of explaining access consciousness with this 'hard problem' of explaining phenomenal consciousness.

So where does the (hard) Problem of Consciousness leave materialism? There is, of course, always the option of rejecting a materialist approach to the mind in favour of substance dualism. But we've already seen that substance dualism has serious problems of its own. A more attractive option is to adopt the *divide-and-conquer* strategy mentioned in chapter 4. On this approach we need two theories: one theory that describes the nature of mental states in general, and another theory that describes conscious experiences in particular. The first theory would need to offer a satisfactory account of all aspects of the mind, bar conscious experience. Here the prospects for materialism are positive. Although neither behaviourism nor identity theory offered wholly successful accounts of the non-conscious mind, functionalism promises to succeed where they failed. The second theory would have to solve the Problem of Consciousness, explaining why we have conscious experiences and why those experiences each feel the way they do. Here materialism's prospects are less positive. As we'll see in the next section, functionalism is no better equipped to solve the problem than the other materialist theories. But this shortcoming means that functionalism is not so much false as incomplete. For a complete picture, functionalism would have to be supplemented by some *non*-functionalist theory of conscious experiences.

So what theory should occupy the second theoretical role of explaining consciousness? Although numerous theories have been offered, increasing attention has been paid to two bold options: property dualism, which says that conscious experiences are non-physical features of the mind; and illusionism, which says that conscious experiences do not exist. In the third section of this chapter, we'll explore both of these radical theories. Before that, though, we must get a better idea of what motivates these theories by taking a closer look at the Problem of Consciousness.

5.2 Three Arguments Against Materialism

Numerous arguments have been offered for thinking that conscious experience cannot be accounted for in terms of physico-functional properties. The three most influential of these are the Zombie Argument, the Spectrum Inversion Argument and the Knowledge Argument. These arguments offer striking thought-experiments designed to show that conscious experiences have non-physical properties.

5.2.1 The Zombie Argument

The notion of a philosophical zombie was introduced by Robert Kirk in the 1970s and later developed by David Chalmers in the 1990s. A zombie is a being that lacks phenomenal consciousness but who acts in all the same ways as a phenomenally conscious being acts. Unlike the zombies you find in a Hollywood film, its behaviour is completely indistinguishable from that of a normal person. If your best friend was a zombie, you wouldn't know. The Zombie Argument against materialism invites you to imagine your own zombie twin. Your zombie twin is a duplicate that's like you in all physical respects, right down to your neurons. It is also like you in all *functional* respects. It processes sensory inputs in the same way as you and produces behavioural outputs in the same way as you. The functional roles that your brain states perform are the same as the functional roles that its brain states perform. Your zombie twin differs from you in only one respect: it has no conscious experiences. When you stub your toe, you say 'Ouch!', hop around and experience a feeling of pain. When your zombie twin stubs its toe, it says 'Ouch!' and hops around, but it feels nothing. When you sip a strong cup of Yorkshire Tea, you say 'Yum!', sit back in your chair and experience a taste of bitterness. When your zombie twin drinks a strong cup of Yorkshire Tea, it says 'Yum!', sits back in its chair and experiences no taste at all. From the *outside*, your zombie twin is exactly like you, but on the *inside* everything is dark.

Interestingly, your zombie twin would still have mental states that are *access* conscious. If your perception of an advert is available for you to report and to guide your reasoning and actions, then the equivalent state of your zombie twin will be similarly available. Access consciousness is a functional notion, so your perfect functional duplicate will have all the same access conscious states that you have. But having access to a mental state is one thing and *experiencing* it is quite another.

The zombie thought-experiment is meant to show us that zombies are metaphysically possible. The word 'metaphysically' is important here. Even if something is impossible given the actual laws of nature, it can still be metaphysically possible. A perfect circle, for example, might be impossible, given how the world is actually set up. But perfect circles are still metaphysically possible in so far as they could exist if the laws of nature were different. A square circle, by contrast, is impossible no matter what laws of nature you change. Zombie twins might well be impossible, given the actual laws of nature, but the thought-experiment is meant to suggest that they are nonetheless possible in this broader metaphysical sense.

The problem for materialist theories is that they are committed to the metaphysical impossibility of zombies. If materialism is true, then someone like you in all physical respects must be like you in all mental respects. But your zombie twin is someone like you in all physical respects but who differs from you mentally in that they lack consciousness. Functionalism defines mental states in terms of functional properties rather than physical properties and faces much the same problem. If functionalism is true, then two beings that are functionally alike must be mentally alike. But your zombie twin is like you in all functional respects, yet not like you in all mental respects. Here's the Zombie Argument in full:

P1. Zombie twins are conceivable.
P2. What is conceivable is possible.
P3. If zombie twins are possible, then materialism is false.
C. Therefore, materialism is false.

Let's take the argument step by step. Why think that zombies are conceivable? Some people agree straight-away that zombies are conceivable. They imagine someone who's their perfect physico-functional duplicate, then imagine that person lacking any experiences. Job done! Others might need to build up to the idea of zombie twins in stages. One way of doing this is by appealing to *real-life* cases where people seem to be missing some aspect of conscious experience. Blindsight is a condition in which subjects suffer damage to part of the brain's visual system and appear to be blind. In the majority of cases, the damage is limited to one hemisphere of the brain, rendering the subject blind in one half of their visual field. If they are presented with a ball in the 'blind' half of the field and asked to state what colour it is, they reply that they cannot see it. But the fascinating thing about blindsight is this: if the subject is asked to *guess* what colour the ball is, they will generally guess correctly. This means there is a sense in which the subject *can* see the ball. One way to make sense of this is to suggest that the subject perceives things in the 'blind' area without having the *conscious experience* of seeing. They can do at least some of the things that sighted people can do, but on the inside their visual experience of that region is dark. They have certain perceptual states, but there is nothing it's like for them to have those perceptual states.

If you can understand this interpretation of the real-life phenomenon of blindsight, we can use this as a starting point for conceiving of zombies. Imagine that our subject starts to adapt to their condition. They still don't have a visual experience of things in that region, but when asked what colour the ball is, they now give their answer without hesitation. They don't report being blind in that region and give no indication that, from their perspective, they are guessing what colour the ball is. In fact, they get so good at this that their behaviour is indistinguishable from that of someone who is fully sighted. If asked whether they are having a conscious experience of the ball, they would answer yes, even though they are not. Now imagine that our subject has blindsight not just in one half of the visual field but across their whole visual field, and that the condition affects not just their sight but *all* of their senses. And now do the same for all other aspects of their mental life: when they are angry, they do what angry people do but without the feeling of anger; when they desire tea, they do what people who desire tea do but without any experience of desire. Bit by bit, remove all aspects of their conscious experience whilst keeping their functional properties constant. Congratulations! You've now conceived a zombie! To conceive of your zombie twin you just need to imagine yourself with this ramped-up version of blindsight.

Now let's consider P2. Is what is *conceivable* a good guide to what's *possible*? On the one hand, there seems to be a tight link between conceivability and possibility. I can conceive of a polka-dotted square because something being both square and polka-dotted is possible. And a round square is inconceivable precisely because it's impossible. Trying to entertain different scenarios is how we work out what *could have been* and what *cannot be*. On the other hand, there are clear cases where using conceivability as a test for possibility fails. As discussed in chapter 2, one might be able to conceive of J. K. Rowling meeting Robert Galbraith, not knowing that such a thing is impossible because they're actually the same person. Similarly, Descartes found it inconceivable that a machine could hold a conversation, yet such a thing is actually possible. Conceivability and possibility thus come apart.

Where does this leave us with conceivability tests? One option is to say that conceivability *never* justifies conclusions about what's possible. This would allow materialists to brush off the Zombie Argument. But it would commit them to disregarding conceivability tests across the board, which is a hard position to sustain. A more modest option is to say that conceivability *is* a meaningful test of possibility but not a *perfect* one. Like many tests, it sometimes gives us the wrong answer but can still be a useful guide to the truth when used appropriately.

How then can we determine whether a conceivability test has misfired? Well, one of the main things that cause trouble is not knowing all the facts relevant to the scenario you're trying to conceive. If I had all the relevant facts about Rowling at my disposal, I would know that Rowling went to the publishers and said 'I want to write under the pseudonym Robert Galbraith', and that she sat writing the books that would later be published under that name. Knowing these facts, it would become *inconceivable* that Rowling could meet Galbraith. So although it was prima facie conceivable that Rowling could meet Galbraith, it is not conceivable under *ideal* conditions, i.e. conditions under which I have all the relevant facts at my disposal. Something similar goes for Descartes. Descartes didn't know that machines could be designed to process information in complex ways, and if he *had* known this, then a linguistically competent machine would not have been inconceivable to him.

This shifts the dialectic around the Zombie Argument. Plausibly, if something is ideally conceivable, then it is possible. So if zombies are ideally conceivable, then the argument is back on track. So why think that zombies are ideally conceivable? The driving thought here is that learning new facts about physico-functional states of the brain won't make any difference to the conceivability of zombies. Facts about our neural connections or about how we process information are simply the *wrong kind* of fact to entail the presence of conscious experience. There is no physico-functional process in the brain the discovery of which could make us say, 'Oh! Now I know about *that* property I can see that my physico-functional state *has* to give rise to a conscious experience'. For any such state, it will always be conceivable for someone to be in that state without being conscious. So even though there's a lot we don't know about our brain states and the functional state they realize, perhaps we can be confident that learning about them will leave the Problem of Consciousness untouched.

With a bit of refinement, P1 and P2 of the Zombie Argument can be defended. P3 states that if materialism is true, then zombies are impossible, which is a straightforward commitment of materialism. And from P1–3 the conclusion follows that materialism is false. More specifically, the argument suggests that materialism fails to explain *conscious experience*. Non-experiential aspects of the mind are not vulnerable to the Zombie

Argument. Try to imagine someone who is like you in all physico-functional respects but who doesn't believe that water is drinkable. It's hard to make sense of someone who says 'water is drinkable', drinks water and generally treats water the same way you do but who *doesn't* believe that water is drinkable. Such a duplicate is inconceivable because beliefs really are functional properties – properties that perfect functional duplicates must share. Since the duplicate has a state that does all the things your belief does, what more could you possibly want for it to qualify as the same belief? In line with the divide-and-conquer approach, the Zombie Argument counts against any materialist theory of phenomenal consciousness but is quite consistent with a materialist theory of non-phenomenal mental states. So there is no threat here to materialist functionalism playing the *first* theoretical role, even if it can't play the second.

5.2.2 The Spectrum Inversion Argument

The Problem of Consciousness is that a person's conscious experience (or lack thereof) does not seem to be fixed by their physical and functional states. The zombie scenario is one way of highlighting this disconnect between the physico-functional and the phenomenally conscious, but a host of other thought-experiments have been introduced that suggest the same thing. One such thought-experiment is the *spectrum inversion* scenario. This argument goes back as far as John Locke (1632–1704) but its recent champions include philosophers such as Martine Nida-Rümelin.

Consider the experience you have as you look at a bowl of fruit. There's a sort of reddish quality that you experience the strawberries as having and a greenish quality that you experience the lime as having. But now imagine 'inverts' who experience things differently. The colour qualities we experience are on a spectrum, but for the invert this spectrum is *reversed*. For any colour quality you experience, an invert would experience the quality at the opposite end of the spectrum. When an invert sees a strawberry, she experiences the quality that you experience when you see a lime. And when she sees a lime, she experiences the quality that you experience when you see a strawberry. Now imagine your 'invert twin', a being like you in all physical and functional respects but whose visual experience of colour is inverted relative to your own. Your invert twin can distinguish things of different colours just as well as you do and would label strawberries as 'red' and limes as 'green'. But on the inside, your invert twin's mental life is very different to yours. This gives us a Spectrum Inversion Argument against materialism that closely parallels the Zombie Argument:

P1. Invert twins are conceivable.
P2. What is conceivable is possible.
P3. If invert twins are possible, then materialism is false.
C. Therefore, materialism is false.

P2 and P3 work in just the same way as the corresponding premises of the Zombie Argument. But what about P1's claim that invert twins are indeed conceivable? It might again be helpful to build up to the idea using actual cases. People perceive colour in subtly different ways. Chromosomal differences mean that women and men are sensitive to wavelengths in slightly different ways, with the result that women generally perceive colours as slightly darker than men do. In most contexts, this difference between men and women would not be manifest in behaviour. They would sort colours in the same kind of way and label the same things as red, green and so on. Yet their visual experiences would be subtly different.

This difference in visual experience is connected to a slight difference at the functional level: careful experiments reveal some observable differences in how women and men categorize colours. But in other cases there might be *no* functional difference between two people who experience colours differently. Martine Nida-Rümelin highlights possible real-life cases of spectrum inversion. Colour perception depends on cone cells in the retina. There are three kinds of cone cell, and each kind is more sensitive to a different band of wavelength – red, green and blue wavelengths respectively. This difference in sensitivity is explained by the different 'photopigments' contained in each cell. When we see a red object, each cone is affected by the red wavelengths to different degrees. The red-detecting cone, for instance, will be much more affected than the blue-detecting cone. So by tracking the *differences* between how the three kinds of cone are affected, the visual system can work out what colour things are.

Red–green colour blindness is the result of a genetic trait that causes the red-detecting and green-detecting cones to have the *same* kind of photopigment, meaning that there's no difference in how much the red-detecting cones and green-detecting cones are affected by red wavelengths. But a rare combination of genetic factors (affecting an estimated 14 in every 10,000 men) causes these photopigments to be *inverted* relative to the normal eye. The red-detecting cones contain a green-sensitive photopigment and the green-detecting cones contain a red-sensitive photopigment. Red wavelengths would thus affect the green-detecting cones *more* than they affect the red-detecting cones. Now, the amazing thing about this anomaly is that it does not affect one's ability to discriminate colours. Unlike with colour blindness, the *difference* in activation of the cone types is still there. This makes it a live possibility that these people are functionally indistinguishable from ordinary people but with spectrum-inverted visual experiences. Yet if functionalism is true, such a thing should be impossible. From here, it's not such an imaginative leap to conceive of someone like you in all functional and physical respects (including their retinas) but who nonetheless has visual experiences that are inverted relative to your own.

The Zombie Argument and the Spectrum Inversion Argument draw attention to different aspects of the Problem of Consciousness. The Zombie Argument suggests that materialism cannot explain why you are phenomenally conscious. The Spectrum Inversion Argument suggests that materialism cannot explain why your phenomenal consciousness is the particular way that it is. It is one thing to explain where conscious experiences come from and another thing to explain what those conscious experiences are like. The specific features that characterize our conscious experiences are known as *phenomenal properties*. Mindy's experience at a specific moment will be characterized by a whole range of phenomenal *properties* – the stinging quality of the pain in her ankle, the greenish quality of the grass and so on. These *properties* make up a subject's *phenomenology* – their ever-changing subjective perspective on the world. And the Spectrum Inversion Argument suggests that our phenomenology is inexplicable in physico-functional terms.

5.2.3 The Knowledge Argument

Imagine a neuroscientist called Mary who has an incredible knowledge of the science behind colour vision. She knows all about how different coloured objects reflect light of different wavelengths and how these wavelengths affect the retina. She knows all about how signals travel down the optic nerve and how these signals are processed by the visual system. And she knows all about how the resulting perceptual states interact with our other mental states and guide our behaviour. And, thanks to advances in science, Mary's scientific knowledge of colour vision is *complete*. In short, she knows *all* the physico-functional facts about colour perception. But here's the catch: she gains all of this knowledge whilst living in a colourless environment. She was born into a black-and-white prison where even her skin was painted grey and she has never seen a colour. She learns all about the science of colour perception from black-and-white textbooks and videos. One day, she escapes from her monochromatic prison and sets eyes on a ripe tomato. And when she does so, she learns a new fact about colour vision: she learns what it's like to experience redness.

What does this thought-experiment tell us about the nature of consciousness? Frank Jackson (1982) introduced this scenario to argue that materialism is false. When Mary sees red for the first time, she learns a fact about conscious experience. But she already knew all of the physical and functional facts about colour perception, and you can't learn something that you already know. So what Mary learns must be a *non*-physical fact about colour perception. Put another way, she already knew about all the physical properties involved in seeing red so what she learns about must be a non-physical property involved in seeing red. That reddish quality you experience when you see red things must be a non-physical property of your perceptual experience. This gives us the following argument:

P1. Before leaving her room, Mary knew all the physical facts about colour perception.
P2. On leaving her room, Mary learns what it's like to experience red.
P3. What it's like to experience red is a fact about colour perception.
C1. Therefore, the fact Mary learns is a non-physical fact.
P4. If materialism is true, there are no non-physical facts.
C2. Therefore, materialism is false.

The first two premises do most of the work in this argument. An assumption of P1 is that Mary could learn all the physico-functional facts about colour vision without experiencing redness. If you think about what the relevant facts are, it's plausible that these facts could be learned in a monochromatic environment. Mary's ignorance of what it's like to experience redness wouldn't preclude her from knowing physical facts about wavelengths, retinas or neurons, nor would it preclude her from knowing functional facts about how colour information is processed. And an assumption of P2 is that Mary couldn't have used her physico-functional knowledge to *work out* what it's like to experience redness. Again, this is plausible if you think about the kinds of fact she has at her disposal. Knowing all those physico-functional facts might put Mary in a position to deduce yet more physico-functional facts, but she couldn't reason herself into having an experience of redness. Even with Mary's complete scientific knowledge, there's nothing about what goes on in the head of someone who sees red that would tell her they're having an experience with a reddish quality rather than an experience with a greenish quality.

As with the previous arguments, the key steps can be motivated using a real-life case. Knut Nordby (1942–2005) was a vision scientist with a rare condition called 'achromatopsia' that caused his retinas to lack the cone cells required for colour vision. Despite this visual impairment, Nordby was able to have a long career as a vision scientist. Nordby could understand and discover scientific facts about vision without needing to have had visual experiences of colour for himself. And, despite his expert knowledge of vision science, he couldn't *deduce* what it would be like to experience redness. Nordby's condition was never cured, but if it *had* been, then he presumably would have learned something about colour perception that his scientific knowledge couldn't have told him. The Mary scenario only varies from the Nordby case in terms of the *amount* of scientific knowledge Mary has (she has all of it instead of lots of it) and the *cause* of her perceptual limitations (she has a mono-chromatic environment instead of a retinal condition). But it's hard to see why either of these differences would mean Mary could work out what it's like to experience redness where Nordby could not.

Critics of the Knowledge Argument object to the move from epistemological claims about what Mary *knows* about colour experiences to a metaphysical conclusion about the actual nature of colour experience. One suggestion is that all the facts about colour experience are physico-functional facts but that there are different *ways* of knowing those facts. So when Mary sees the red rose for the first time, she doesn't learn a new physical fact. Instead, she learns about one of the old physical facts in a new way. Having a visual experience of redness is nothing more than being in a brain state that performs a certain functional role. But by having that brain state *for herself*, Mary gains a new perspective on that physical fact. There are subtle issues here that need to be considered carefully, but one question worth asking is how could Mary possibly gain a new perspective on something that she already knows everything about? Learning that J. K. Rowling is Robert Galbraith could give you a new perspective on somebody you already knew about. However, as discussed above, if you already knew *everything* about J. K. Rowling, then you'd already know about her pseudonym and there would be no room left to take this new perspective on her. The very idea of a new perspective on something implies that there's something about it you don't already know. So if Mary already knows *everything* about the physico-functional state of seeing red, then there would be no room left for her to gain a new perspective on it. Mary could only be *surprised* to discover what it's like to see red if there's more to seeing red than the physico-functional properties she already knows. Like the Spectrum Inversion Argument, the Knowledge Argument suggests that the phenomenal properties of our conscious experiences cannot be accounted for in physico-functional terms.

5.3 Dualism and Illusionism

We've now got a better grip on the Problem of Consciousness. The challenge is to explain why some mental states are phenomenally conscious, and why they have the particular phenomenal properties they have. But the Zombie Argument, Spectrum Inversion Argument and Knowledge Argument suggest that materialism is incapable of providing such an explanation. How should this problem be dealt with? We will focus on two bold proposals: property dualism and illusionism.

Property dualists (e.g. David Chalmers) argue that phenomenal consciousness is constituted by immaterial properties. The solution to the Problem of Consciousness is to reject materialism and add these immaterial properties into our metaphysical picture of reality. Mindy's ankle pain is characterized by various functional properties, such as being caused by certain kinds of stimulation and causing certain kinds of behaviour, but it also has phenomenal properties. Specifically, it has the phenomenal property of being a conscious experience with a certain painful quality. The functional properties of Mindy's pain are explained by physical facts about Mindy's brain state and its interactions with other physical states. But the phenomenal properties have no such physical explanation – they are an additional, non-physical ingredient. Mindy is phenomenally conscious because she has mental states with immaterial phenomenal properties, and she has the particular phenomenology she has because of the particular phenomenal properties of those mental states. Mindy's overall conscious experience is thus constituted by these non-physical phenomenal properties.

Property dualism deals with the three arguments in

the previous section by accepting their anti-materialist conclusions. On this view, zombie twins are possible because your twin could have all the same physico-functional properties as you but without having any of your non-physical phenomenal properties. Similarly, invert twins are possible because your twin could have the same physico-functional properties as you yet have inverted non-physical phenomenal properties. And Mary learns something new on escaping her monochromatic prison because her complete physical knowledge leaves out the non-physical property that characterizes what it's like to experience redness.

How does property dualism differ from substance dualism? The first thing to note is that property dualists are advocates of the divide-and-conquer strategy. Where Descartes thought that *everything* mental is immaterial, the property dualist only thinks that *phenomenal properties* are immaterial. Against Descartes, they hold that non-phenomenal aspects of the mind can be explained in physico-functional terms. The second thing to note is that property dualists posit non-physical properties without positing non-physical *substances*. A substance dualist says that Mindy has both a physical body that is the bearer of her physical properties and an immaterial mind that is the bearer of her mental properties. Property dualists simply say that Mindy has both physical properties and non-physical properties. Despite these differences, though, property dualism and substance dualism agree that the mind can only be accommodated by positing something non-physical.

Illusionists (e.g. Keith Frankish) take a different view and argue that phenomenal consciousness does not exist. The solution to the Problem of Consciousness is that phenomenal consciousness is a sham. Mindy is not phenomenally conscious of her pain because she is not phenomenally conscious of *anything*. And Mindy's pain is not characterized by a phenomenal property of painfulness because there are no such properties. Her

pain is a functional state realized by an underlying physical brain state, and there is nothing more to it. That
said, it *appears* to Mindy as if there is something more
to her pain. When she is in a pain state, it appears to
her that she has a special kind of awareness of a special
kind of property. We are all victim to the illusion that
there is this extra dimension to the mind that cannot
be explained in functional terms. Access consciousness
is still real but this extra thing known as *phenomenal*
consciousness is a myth. The intentionality of mental
states means we can represent things that don't really
exist. Just as you can misrepresent the existence of the
Holy Grail, you can misrepresent the existence of your
own consciousness. It is as if the mind is playing a magic
trick on itself, conjuring up the appearance of these
special phenomenal states. But in reality there is no such
thing as magic – only the illusions that make the magic
appear real.

It is this illusion that makes zombies and inverts appear
conceivable. We take ourselves to have a special kind of
consciousness that cannot be explained functionally and
imagine our zombie twin lacking this consciousness. But
in reality we don't have this magical kind of consciousness, so there is nothing we have that our zombie twin
could lack. Similarly, we take our perceptual experiences
to be characterized by phenomenal properties and imagine an invert twin whose properties are inverted relative
to our own. But in reality our mental states have no
such magical properties, so there is nothing that could
be switched around in our invert twin. Similarly, Mary
doesn't learn anything new on escaping her prison. All
that happens is that she falls victim to an illusion from
which she was previously free: the illusion that perceptions of redness have a special non-physical property
that cannot be captured by her science books.

Crucially, this illusion can itself be explained in functional terms. There is something about some of our
mental states that causes us to think they have a special

non-functional nature. Different illusionists offer different explanations. What unites them is the thought that explaining phenomenal consciousness is like explaining a magic trick: you don't have to explain how the magician levitated; you just have to explain why it *seemed* as if they levitated. Once you've explained why we *seem* to be phenomenally conscious, the job is done. Once you've explained the erroneous *judgements* we make about phenomenal consciousness, there's nothing left to explain. Mary's complete scientific knowledge would tell her why people *think* that their perceptual states have inexplicable qualities, but the qualities themselves would not need explaining as they don't really exist.

Property dualism and illusionism are theories of *phenomenal consciousness* rather than general theories of the mental. Both views can be naturally combined with a functionalist theory of the non-phenomenal. But which of these radical theories should we prefer? Although they are concerned with phenomenal consciousness rather than all aspects of the mind, these theories can still be judged by how plausibly they answer the Three Big Questions.

5.4 Property Dualism, Illusionism and the Three Big Questions

5.4.1 *The Mind and Matter Question*

How does phenomenal consciousness fit into the material world? Put another way, what is the relationship between phenomenal properties and physical properties? Property dualists claim that phenomenal properties are among the basic ingredients of reality. Physicists offer a list of fundamental physical properties – things like charge, mass and spin. But according to the property dualist, this list must be supplemented by non-physical properties such as painfulness, reddishness and bitterness. The complete metaphysical story of the mind then has two halves: a physical side and a non-physical side. Consider Mindy's mind. Mindy has a host of functional states that are realized by physical states of her brain. But if Mindy *only* had those things, she'd be a zombie. She would do and say all the same things, but she wouldn't have any experiences. Mindy's mind is *also* constituted by non-physical properties that combine to create her rich experience of the world, and it is these phenomenal properties that distinguish her from a zombie.

One of the main problems for substance dualism was the causal closure of the physical. The material world of physical properties forms a causally closed system, meaning there's no room for anything non-physical to cause anything in that system that wouldn't have happened anyway. A theory that posits anything non-physical is thus committed to either *epiphenomenalism* or *interactionism*.

On the *epiphenomenalist* route, the non-physical has no causal influence on the physical. For substance dualists, this means that the mind – and all of our mental states – are epiphenomenal. For property dualists, it means that our *phenomenal* properties have no physical effects, while our non-phenomenal mental properties do. Can property dualists just bite the bullet and concede that phenomenal consciousness is causally irrelevant? They could maintain that our behaviour is caused by our mental states and just scrap the idea that our behaviour can specifically be caused by our conscious experience. This path still has some pretty dramatic consequences. It would mean that the conscious experience I have when drinking tea is not what causes me to drink more tea. The experience *occurs* but it doesn't make any difference to my behaviour. My zombie twin's tea-drinking behaviour is explained entirely by physico-functional processes, and *my* tea-drinking behaviour would have exactly the same explanation. The way that drinking tea *feels* to me on the inside would just be a metaphysical sideshow – an irrelevant by-product of processes in the material world. Similarly, Mindy hopping around and saying 'Ouch!' wouldn't be caused by the *feeling* of pain. If the pain had felt like a tickle, she would have behaved in exactly the same way. And her celebration after scoring wouldn't be caused by the *feeling* of elation. Had she felt nothing at all, she would have done just the same thing.

Stranger still, it would mean that the things we say about phenomenal consciousness are in no way caused by our phenomenal consciousness. Utterances like 'I'm phenomenally conscious' or 'The painful quality of my experience is unpleasant' or 'I can conceive of a being like me in all functional respects but who lacks consciousness' are exclusively caused by our physico-functional states. So if you say these things, so would your zombie twin. Similarly, my zombie twin would have written exactly the same chapter on the Problem of Consciousness, despite not being phenomenally conscious. Zombie brains are wired up in such a way that they *misreport* being phenomenally conscious. But according to the property dualist, the same wiring that causes their inaccurate utterances causes your *accurate* utterances. Your phenomenal properties are completely inefficacious yet, by a breathtaking cosmic coincidence, you happen to make statements that accurately describe your conscious experience.

The interactionist route is no less problematic. On this view, any physical event with a non-physical cause will *also* have a sufficient physical cause. For the substance dualist, this means that whenever your behaviour is caused by a mental state, it also has a complete physical cause. For property dualists, such overdetermination only occurs when the mental state in question is phenomenal. This means that property dualism can posit *less* overdetermination than substance dualism. But even this much overdetermination is implausible. Technically speaking, Mindy's painful experience can cause her to hop around and even cause her to say 'the painful quality of my experience is unpleasant'. But here the property dualist must say that she would still have done these things had she not had the painful experience. Because had her experience been absent, a physical cause would still have been sufficient to bring about her behaviour. If our phenomenal states can only achieve this kind of second-rate causal power – the power to cause things that would have happened anyway – it's not clear that the overdetermination route is any better than epiphenomenalism. Like the epiphenomenalist, the interactionist is committed to saying that our consciousness *makes no difference* to our actions. Since interactionism doesn't help out the property dualist, we can put it aside for the rest of the discussion.

Faced with these incredible implications of property dualism, illusionism might start to seem like the more attractive option. Illusionists protect a materialist world view, maintaining that mental states are entirely realized by physical states. It *appears* to us as if there are these extra non-physical things, but these appearances are deceptive. They are no more a threat to physicalism than the illusions of ghosts. Sometimes it seems to us as if something non-physical happens, but when it does we are subject to an illusion that has a completely physical explanation. So with phenomenal properties out of the picture, illusionists can maintain that all *real* aspects of the mind are causally efficacious. There are no mental properties that stand outside the causally closed system of the physical. Their answer to the Mind and Matter Question is that phenomenal properties are an illusion created by purely material minds.

Interestingly, the illusionist and the property dualist agree on more here than it might seem. Both sides think that the statements we make about phenomenal consciousness are not caused by phenomenal properties. Both sides agree that zombies are subject to a cognitive illusion whereby they believe that their mental states have non-physical properties. All they disagree on is whether *we* are zombies: the illusionist says that we are all zombies under the cognitive illusion that we are something more, where the property dualist says that we are all conscious beings who happen to have the phenomenal states that our zombie twins misattribute to themselves. Given that both sides agree that our statements about phenomenal consciousness are the result of cognitive trickery, it's hard to see how property dualism can come out on top. Imagine two people who've just seen a performance where a magician appears to levitate. At first they both think that real magic was involved, then they discover that the apparent levitation was caused by the movement of an ingenious hidden prop. The first person now concludes that the levitation was an illusion and that the performance didn't involve magic after all. But the second person maintains that although the apparent levitation was caused by the hidden prop, it *also* involved real magic. This second position is at best very uncomfortable. By conceding that our phenomenal properties do not make a difference to our beliefs about phenomenal properties, the property dualist inadvertently undermines their reasons for thinking that phenomenal properties exist.

At this point it might look like illusionism has the upper hand, but let's not forget what it means to deny the existence of phenomenal properties. A problem for property dualists was that they deny that our behaviour is caused by the conscious experiences we are having. Well, illusionists deny this too. My continuing tea consumption isn't caused by my conscious experience of tea drinking because there are no such experiences, and Mindy's 'Ouch!' isn't caused by the painful quality she experiences because there is no such quality. As counterintuitive implications go, this is a big one. So *neither* view seems able to accommodate the simple thought that our actions are sometimes the result of our phenomenal states.

5.4.2 The Knowledge Question

Property dualists also run into difficulties with the epistemology of phenomenal properties. How can you know that the quality that Mindy experiences when she looks at grass is the same as the quality you experience when you look at grass? If the visual qualities of Mindy's experience were inverted, you'd have no way of knowing. In fact, her experience might be characterized by qualities you've never even experienced. Worse still, she might not have any conscious experiences at all. How could we know that Mindy isn't a zombie? By definition, Mindy is outwardly indistinguishable from her zombie twin. We can't *perceive* Mindy's phenomenal states, and nothing in her behaviour could show that she is conscious. Issues surrounding phenomenal-to-physical causation make matters even worse. If Mindy's conscious experiences *make no difference* to what Mindy does – whether because of epiphenomenalism or overdetermination – then we have no real evidence that Mindy is phenomenally conscious. In fact, we have no real evidence that *anyone* else is phenomenally conscious.

At least you know what *your* conscious experiences feel like and that *you're* not a zombie. Or do you? If there's a conscious version of you and a zombie version of you, what makes you so sure that you're not the zombie? It certainly *seems* as if you're phenomenally conscious, but there's a sense in which it seems to your zombie twin that it is conscious. After all, your zombie twin would report being conscious and act in all the ways someone acts if they think they have conscious experiences. This means that even if you *are* in fact phenomenally conscious, there might be no way of *knowing* that you are. You have the belief that you are phenomenally conscious, and this belief would be accurate but it would only be accurate as a matter of luck. Your belief is caused by a non-phenomenal physico-functional process, and your phenomenal states make no difference to what you believe. So even though the belief happens to be true, it shouldn't qualify as *knowledge*. If I form a belief about tomorrow's lottery numbers and that belief happens to be true, that wouldn't mean I *knew* what the lottery numbers would be. But your belief that you're conscious would be no better than my belief about the lottery. Or, for a more direct comparison, imagine if the magician who performed the levitation trick really was magic. He has made a career of creating clever illusions but, unbeknownst to him, he has magical abilities that he has never used. So an observer who sees the trick and concludes that the magician has genuine magical abilities would be *right*. But it would be absurd to say that the observer *knows* that the magician has real magical abilities because these abilities are completely irrelevant to why the observer formed that belief.

Property dualism thus has serious trouble with knowledge of other people's conscious experiences and even with knowledge of one's own conscious experiences. Illusionists avoid all this trouble by denying that we know *anything* about phenomenal consciousness because there's simply nothing to know. Once you've denied the existence of ghosts, you don't then have to provide an epistemology of ghosts because the whole point is there are no ghosts for you to know about. There's no need to account for how you know that Mindy's experience of grass has the same phenomenal property as your experience of grass because *neither* of you really experience a phenomenal property. There's no need to account for how you rule out the possibility that Mindy is a zombie because she really is a zombie. And there's no need to account for how you know you're not a zombie because you are! All our beliefs about phenomenal consciousness are the product of an illusion and, like most beliefs caused by illusions, they are false.

When we start thinking about the epistemology of phenomenal consciousness, a difficulty for illusionism begins to emerge. It seems that the *way* we know about our own consciousness precludes the possibility that the whole thing is a trick. Consider a magic trick where it *seems* as if there's a ghost in the theatre when actually there's just a clever trick of the light. The illusion involves a mismatch between two things: the way things *appear* to be (i.e. the apparent presence of a ghost) and the way things *really are* (i.e. the actual absence of a ghost). But now consider the claim that your pain experience is an illusion. This would mean that you *seem* to be having a pain experience when you are not. And this would involve a mismatch between two things: the appearance of having a pain experience and the actual absence of a pain experience. But with phenomenal consciousness, the distinction between appearance and reality has no application. Your pain experiences don't *appear* to you via something else. Rather, a pain experience *is* an appearance. More generally, your phenomenal consciousness is how you experience things as being. When we experience something as being there when it isn't, we are subject to an illusion. But how can we experience *our experience* as being there when it is not? We're just *too close* to our experiences to be misled about them. The only way you can seem to yourself to be having a conscious experience is by *actually having* a conscious experience, so the possibility of a mismatch is foreclosed. On this view, the *way* that we know about our own phenomenal states is such that we can rule out the possibility of illusionism without any further thought. Overall, then, neither property dualism nor illusionism can answer the Knowledge Question straightforwardly.

5.4.3 The Distribution Question

In previous chapters, we considered the distribution of minds. Here, though, our concern is with the distribution of *conscious* minds, i.e. minds that have inner experiences as opposed to zombie minds. When we're investigating what kind of minds things have, the question of whether they're phenomenally conscious is of central importance. If we're wondering about animal minds, for instance, one of the most important questions is whether the animal in question undergoes *experiences*. If we discovered that an octopus has brain states that perform the functional roles of beliefs, desires, memories and so on, that would be a valuable result. But what we *really* want to know is whether the octopus experiences anything and, if it does, what its experiences are like. Similarly, determining that a robot has mental states would be a big deal, but what would be a *really* big deal is determining that robots have *conscious* mental states.

Questions about the distribution of consciousness are of special ethical significance. The question of whether an octopus or a robot deserves our ethical concern is bound up with the question of whether they are phenomenally conscious. After all, if these beings are just zombies, then they cannot experience suffering, and if they cannot experience suffering, perhaps we don't have to worry about 'harming' them. Relatedly, questions about the distribution of consciousness are important to how we see our place in the world. We can be fairly confident that human minds are not the only minds in the world. But might human minds be the only *conscious* minds in the world? If so, we have a special place in the natural order. And if not, we should be keen to learn which other beings have made it into the consciousness club.

Illusionism and property dualism offer surprising answers to the Distribution Question. Illusionists claim that *nothing* is phenomenally conscious. They regard the question itself as a pseudo-question akin to questions about the distribution of magic. There is a different question that illusionists *do* think is worth answering: what is the distribution of the *illusion* of consciousness? Is the illusion of consciousness a uniquely human predicament or are other animals subject to a similar illusion? Might a suitably sophisticated AI end up falling under this illusion and start saying things like 'My awareness cannot be explained in terms of digital processing on a silicon chip'? Answering these questions would certainly mark an important division between different kinds of mind, but it would be a long way from the division with which we started. According to the illusionist, there simply is no division between minds that experience the world and minds of zombies because *all* minds are zombie minds.

Property dualists seem to have some flexibility regarding the distribution of consciousness. Once they have posited non-physical phenomenal properties, they can weigh up different theoretical considerations to decide how these properties are distributed. However, a number of considerations push property dualists towards the conclusion that consciousness is *everywhere*. This is known as *panpsychist* property dualism. For property dualists, phenomenal properties are fundamental non-physical properties that are among the basic building blocks of reality. This makes it very difficult to claim that phenomenal properties are localized to human beings and perhaps some non-human animals. To maintain such a localized view of the distribution of phenomenal properties, property dualists would have to say that these fundamental properties only appeared when beings with sufficiently complex brains evolved. The idea of a fundamental property only springing into existence so recently in the history of the universe is already implausible. But it's even more implausible to think that reality is set up in such a way that brains have this special ability to trigger the occurrence of non-physical properties. Brains are not fundamental constituents of reality. They are complex organs constituted by billions of neurons that are themselves constituted by billions of particles, and they developed as the result of a blind process of natural selection stretching over millennia.

A law of nature connecting the occurrence of phenomenal properties to the presence of a brain is thus no better than a law of nature connecting the occurrence of phenomenal properties to the presence of Jaffa Cakes. Brains and Jaffa Cakes just aren't the kinds of thing that get a special mention in the laws of nature.

To avoid giving organic brains this ad hoc privileged status in the world, the property dualist must instead say that there's nothing special about brains. Our brains are accompanied by non-physical phenomenal properties because *everything* is. Like other basic features of the universe, phenomenal properties can be found in all places and at all times. Besides their mass and extension, photons and electrons have a little bit of consciousness. It's not like *our* rich and complex conscious experiences, but there is something simple that it's like to be an electron. Mindy's conscious experience is made up from these all-pervading phenomenal properties. Just as Mindy only has mass because the fundamental entities from which she is constituted have mass, so too Mindy only has phenomenal consciousness because the fundamental entities from which she is constituted have phenomenal properties.

A particularly elegant version of panpsychism, inspired by Bertrand Russell, claims that phenomenal properties do not exist alongside the physical properties described by physics but instead *underwrite* those properties. Physics describes what fundamental physical entities *do* but does not thereby describe what those things *are*. Charge, spin and mass are a bit like functional roles in the vast physical system of the universe. And, as we know from our discussion of functionalism, functional roles must be *realized* by something. Perhaps, then, phenomenal properties are the realizers of these functional roles. Thinkers such as Mørch have argued exactly this. They propose that physics reveals what these properties do from the outside, and that conscious experience reveals their nature from the inside. Notice that this proposal isn't really a form of property dualism anymore. Instead, it offers a monist view on which the physical and the phenomenal are just two aspects of the same kind of property.

Panpsychism sounds like it should avoid the problems faced by illusionism. On inspection, however, it is not so different. What we were looking for was a *division* between the conscious and the non-conscious. But like illusionism, panpsychist property dualism says there is no such division. *Everything* is conscious and *nothing* is a zombie, so that all-important dividing line isn't there. The important ethical questions about the distribution of consciousness are completely confounded because now conscious experience is everywhere.

Furthermore, this panpsychist view still doesn't tell us which *complex* entities are conscious. Mindy is made up of conscious ingredients that come together to form her own conscious experience. A table is made of conscious ingredients that, presumably, do not come together in such a way – the table itself does not have any conscious experiences. So even if we allow that an octopus is constituted by conscious ingredients, there remains the further question of whether those ingredients add up to the octopus having conscious experiences. The same goes for a bee, a Martian or a self-driving car. There are two sides to this problem. First, there's the epistemological problem of working out which complex beings have conscious experiences. Since phenomenal properties are unobservable non-physical properties, it's unclear how this question could ever be answered. Second, there's the metaphysical problem of how basic phenomenal properties are meant to add up to produce complex conscious experiences at all. Unless there's some kind of phenomenal chemistry governing how these properties combine, complex conscious experiences will remain inexplicable.

5.5 Some Final Thoughts on Consciousness

It should now be clear that property dualism and illusionism are pretty radical proposals. Faced with these extremes, shouldn't we explore the possibility of a middle-ground position with less counter-intuitive implications? There are hordes of theories that attempt to do just this, but these theories seem to fall foul of familiar problems. Some theories offer new ways of *explaining* consciousness in physico-functional terms. But these theories always seem to leave an unexplained residue, which takes us back to the dualist/illusionist dilemma. Other theories concede that consciousness *cannot* be explained in physico-functional terms but maintain that conscious experiences are just brain states on which we have a special point of view. But when they try to explain this point of view, they too leave something out, leading us once more to the dualist/illusionist dilemma.

There is a simple explanation for why such theories fail: phenomenal properties are not the kind of thing that can fit into a materialist metaphysical picture, so you've either got to admit that they are non-physical or deny their existence altogether. There is thus a sense in which property dualists and illusionists, despite their fundamental disagreement, agree on something important about phenomenal properties. They agree that phenomenal properties cannot be physical. What they disagree on is what to infer from this: the property dualists conclude that phenomenal properties are therefore non-physical, while the illusionists infer that phenomenal properties are therefore non-existent.

One of the only ways I see out of this dilemma is to rethink how the Problem of Consciousness is framed. The problem concerns the relationship between consciousness and the physical world. The default assumption has always been that the problem will be solved by probing the consciousness end of the equation. And this is exactly what property dualists and illusionists do – they make radical claims about the nature of consciousness designed to resolve the problem. But a better strategy might be to focus on the physical end of the equation. Debates around the Problem of Consciousness tend to assume that we already have a good grip on the nature of matter. But philosophers such as Barbara Montero (2001) have argued that this confidence is ill-founded. Until we really understand the nature of physical things, how can we be sure that phenomenal consciousness can't be explained in physical terms?

One promising version of this strategy is to build on the insight from Russell briefly mentioned earlier. Russell suggested that science describes the causal roles that physical entities play but does not describe the underlying nature of those entities. If Russell is right, there's an identifiable blind spot in our knowledge of the physical – a known unknown. And rather than standing outside the causally closed system described by science, these unknown properties would *constitute* that system. As we saw, one option is to say that this blind spot is filled with phenomenal properties and that consciousness pervades the universe. A more modest suggestion is that this blind spot is filled with properties that are non-phenomenal but integral to the explanation of consciousness. On this view, the apparent inexplicability of consciousness merely reflects our ignorance of the physical processes from which consciousness emerges. If we could only get a grip on the full nature of the physical, the Problem of Consciousness would disappear.

Key Concepts

Access consciousness: a mental state is access conscious when it is available for use by one's wider mental processes, such as reasoning and the guidance of speech and action.

Illusionism: the theory that the existence of phenomenal properties is illusory.

Panpsychism: the view that everything has phenomenal properties.

Phenomenal consciousness: to be phenomenally conscious is to have subjective experiences. A mental state is phenomenally conscious if there is something it's like to be in that state for its subject.

Phenomenal properties: these properties characterize what our phenomenally conscious experiences are like, e.g. the painful quality of a headache.

Property dualism: the theory that phenomenal properties are non-physical properties.

Spectrum inverted twin: a being like you in all physical and functional respects but whose conscious experiences have phenomenal properties that are inverted relative to your own.

The Problem of Consciousness: the problem of explaining phenomenal consciousness in physico-functional terms. Known as the 'hard' problem to contrast it with the more tractable problem of explaining access consciousness.

Zombie twin: a hypothetical being like you in all physical and functional respects but who lacks phenomenal consciousness.

References and Further Reading

- David J. Chalmers, 'Consciousness and its Place in Nature', in David J. Chalmers (ed.) (2021), *Philosophy of Mind: Classical and Contemporary Readings*, 2nd edn, New York: Oxford University Press. In this article, Chalmers offers a valuable overview of the different responses to the Problem of Consciousness, including a summary of Block's distinction between access and phenomenal consciousness.
- David J. Chalmers (1997), 'Moving Forward on the

Problem of Consciousness', *Journal of Consciousness Studies* 4(1): 3–46. Here Chalmers puts forward his version of the Zombie Argument and proposes that phenomenal properties are non-physical properties.

- Frank Jackson (1982), 'Epiphenomenal Qualia', *Philosophical Quarterly* 32: 127–36. Reprinted in Chalmers, *Philosophy of Mind*, op. cit. This paper introduces the famous case of Mary the neuroscientist.
- Martine Nida-Rümelin (1996), 'Pseudonormal Vision: An Actual Case of Qualia Inversion?', *Philosophical Studies* 82(2): 145–57. Reprinted in Chalmers, *Philosophy of Mind*, op. cit. Nida-Rümelin builds on real-life cases to argue that spectrum inverts may be among us.
- Hedda Hassel Mørch (2017), 'Is Matter Conscious?', *Nautilus* 47: 90–6. Reprinted in Chalmers, *Philosophy of Mind*, op. cit. Mørch makes a case for panpsychism, arguing that phenomenal properties underwrite basic physical properties.
- K. Frankish (2016), 'Illusionism as a Theory of Consciousness', *Journal of Consciousness Studies* 23(11–12): 11–39. Reprinted in Chalmers, *Philosophy of Mind*, op. cit. This paper argues that we should deny the existence of conscious experience.
- Barbara Montero (2001), 'Post-Physicalism', *Journal of Consciousness Studies* 8(2): 61–80. Reprinted in Chalmers, *Philosophy of Mind*, op. cit. Montero makes a persuasive case for thinking that we've been framing the Problem of Consciousness in the wrong way and that we must re-examine what we really know about the physical.

6

The Mind Today

6.1 The Interdisciplinary Study of the Mind

As we have seen, the philosophy of mind has always had an interesting relationship with science. Descartes sought to understand how the mind could fit into the emerging scientific picture of the natural world. Behaviourists and identity theorists drew inspiration from science to address long-standing philosophical questions about the mental. And the computer revolution, with its subtle interplay of philosophical and scientific insights, gave rise to the functionalist theory that still dominates philosophy of mind today. But this long history of *interactions* between scientific and philosophical research has now morphed into a genuine *integration* of the different disciplines.

Philosophers often play an active role in interpreting psychological findings and in determining the direction of new research. And psychological findings play a central role in deciding old philosophical questions and in generating new questions for philosophical discussion. Interdisciplinary conferences that bring philosophers and cognitive scientists together are now commonplace, as are interdisciplinary research projects on which philosophers and cognitive scientists collaborate on a shared study of the mind. This is not to say that the division between the philosophy and science of the mind has disappeared entirely: philosophers still have different goals and different methods to scientists, and there remain some philosophers of mind who confront deep questions about the mind without engaging with science at all. Nevertheless, philosophy and the cognitive sciences have never been more integrated.

One factor in this integration is the presence of functionalism as a shared framework for thinking about the mind. Mainstream psychology takes a broadly functional approach to the mind, characterizing mental states in terms of how they interact with sensory inputs, behavioural outputs and other mental states. You might not find many psychologists explicitly endorsing the functionalist claim that mental properties are functional properties realized by physical states, but that's because psychologists aren't in the business of explicitly stating their philosophical outlooks. Implicitly, though, much psychological research is guided by the assumption that mental states are distinguished by their functional role. The same goes for work in artificial intelligence. When researchers aim to create artificial minds with beliefs, desires, intentions and so on, what they are aiming to create are artificial minds with states that *function* in the way that beliefs, desires and intentions function. Of course, there are many philosophers of mind who object to functionalism and many psychologists who adopt a non-functionalist approach to the study of the mind. Even so, functionalism's status as the leading paradigm in both philosophy and the cognitive sciences has provided a shared framework for discussion, even among those who challenge the paradigm.

Philosophers of mind have spent considerable time trying to understand how different kinds of mental representation work, how states of the brain can constitute mental representations and whether all mental states are mental representations. Indeed, representationalists argue that the different types of mental state are distinguished by their representational properties. Mindy's perceptual state is the kind of mental state it is because of what it represents (the ball) and how it represents it (perceptually). Other mental states can represent the same thing in different ways (e.g. a belief about the ball) or represent different things in the same way (e.g. a perception of the grass). And, as we touched on in chapter 4, these representational features of mental states could well be explained in terms of their functional role.

Mental representation has also been a central concern of cognitive scientists. Cognitive psychologists have explored how mental representations function, neuroscientists have explored how the brain encodes mental representations, and AI researchers have developed various different ways for computers to represent the world, including self-driving cars guided by sophisticated representations of their environment. This shared concern for mental representation has made it a hot topic of interdisciplinary debate. Do we really need mental representations to explain our behaviour, or are there non-representational explanations that can do the job? What kinds of representation are different animals capable of? For instance, does a bee navigate using an internal representation of its environment and does a plant that follows the sun represent the time of day? Are computer representations really representations or do a computer's states only represent in so far as we *give* them meaning? Answering these questions requires the careful integration of abstract philosophical questions about the nature of intentionality and mentality with concrete empirical questions about how different biological and artificial beings function. This remains a lively area of research today.

Another area of shared concern is phenomenal consciousness. Historically, the cognitive sciences have ignored phenomenal consciousness in favour of those aspects of the mind that better lend themselves to scientific investigation. But now, thanks to the influence of philosophy, cognitive scientists recognize conscious experience as a topic that cannot be ignored. Consciousness has become a target of serious scientific inquiry and sophisticated experimental methods have been developed for exploring conscious experience in a systematic and objective manner. Many scientists have even grappled directly with questions about the metaphysics of consciousness. Some have gone down the illusionist route and proposed scientific accounts of why we are under the illusion that our mental states have inexplicable phenomenal properties. Others have gone down the property dualist route and proposed theories on which information states in the brain are correlated with non-physical phenomenal states. Independent of the merit of such views, the very fact that they are being proposed indicates the welcome integration of philosophical thought into scientific practice.

Mental representation and phenomenal consciousness are big topics of interdisciplinary interest. But there's also a whole host of more specific topics that philosophers and scientists have explored in tandem. Each type of mental state discussed in this book has been the target of focused interdisciplinary inquiry, with valuable work on the nature of perception, emotion, intention, belief, desire, imagination, attention and action. Research has also targeted some more elusive varieties of mental state that are not part of our common-sense picture of the mind. 'Implicit biases', for example, are an important variety of mental state posited to explain a range of empirical findings. An implicit bias is a *stereotype* that influences how we interpret the world. Crucially, the content of an implicit bias can go against what you actually believe. Someone who doesn't hold racist beliefs, for example, may still have an implicit bias against members of a racial group. Philosophers have helped shed light on the nature and significance of these biases and on the measures we should take to counteract them. Interdisciplinary attention has also been given to important topics in psychiatry. For example, there are various disorders of self-awareness in which the ordinary boundaries between self and world are distorted or lost. Understanding these disorders has required not just the careful scientific investigation of behavioural patterns and neural processes but the careful philosophical investigation of the nature of self-awareness, the structure of self-knowledge and the metaphysics of the self.

6.2 The Three Big Questions Today

To appreciate how philosophy of mind looks today, we can look again at our Three Big Questions and consider how recent work has generated insightful new proposals and interesting new lines of inquiry.

6.2.1 The Mind and Matter Question

Many still hold that mental states are functional states that are *realized* by physical states. However, some researchers have argued that we need to change our assumptions about the physical states that perform these functional roles. The default assumption has been that the realizers of human mental states are *brain states*. For a robot or a particularly unusual animal, things might be different, but *our* mental states are realized by neural states. On this view, the brain is the hardware on which the software of the human mind runs. This assumption has come under increasing pressure. One school of thought argues that our mental processes stretch beyond the brain and include the body. Susan Hurley (1954–2007) argued that there are no good reasons to think that mental processes have to happen *between* a sensory input being received and a bodily output being produced. Instead, these processes can reach out beyond the skull to include our bodies. When you count on your fingers, for example, your hand movements are literally part of the mental process of counting. And when Mindy plays football, her actions are guided by what's happening in her whole body – the reactions of her muscles, the pangs in her stomach – and not just by what's going on in her head. On this view, our mental processes are *embodied* processes. Mental states are still defined by their functional roles, but these roles are performed not just by brain states but by a wider physical system that encompasses various other states of the body. After all, one of the key lessons of functionalism is that mental processes are *multiply realizable*, so the suggestion that our own mental processes are realized by more than just the brain cannot be dismissed lightly.

Another school of thought pushes this idea further and suggests that the physical realizers of our mental states extend beyond the body. Clark and Chalmers (1998) argued for this 'Extended Mind thesis' using an intriguing thought-experiment. They invite us to imagine two people – Otto and Inga – both of whom are travelling to a museum. Otto has Alzheimer's disease and has compensated for his memory difficulties by writing the directions down on a notepad that he carries with him. Inga, on the other hand, has an internal memory of the route to the museum stored in her brain. Does Otto remember where the museum is? Clark and Chalmers argue that he does. Something is a memory in virtue of the functional role that it plays. The relevant state of Inga's brain functions in such a way that it constitutes a memory of where the museum is. But Otto's notepad plausibly plays the *same* functional role and so ought to qualify as a memory too. In particular, both Otto and Inga's memories function to support beliefs about the location of the museum. If asked where the museum is,

Inga would consult her internally stored memory and answer '53rd Street'. And if asked the same question, Otto would consult his externally stored memory and give the same answer. We might have an intuitive resistance to a person's memory being stored on ink and paper rather than in neural structures, but such intuitions are not to be trusted. We've already acknowledged that beings with brains completely different to ours can have the same kind of mental state as us, so what principled reason could we have for denying that Otto's notepad contains his memory?

Critics of these *embodied* and *extended* views of the mental have argued that things external to the brain can *influence* what happens in our mind but can never be *constituents* of mental processes. This has raised important new questions about the nature of the mental and the relationship between mind and matter. One strand of the debate concerns how narrow or broad the functional characterization of a mental state type should be. All sides agree that Otto's notepad doesn't function *exactly* like Inga's brain state. For instance, Inga's brain state can directly cause her to form beliefs about the museum's location, whereas Otto's notepad can only generate these beliefs if Otto looks at it. The question is whether the similarities in function are enough for Otto's notepad to qualify as a memory. On a broad characterization of the memory role, it would qualify, and on a narrow characterization it might not. As we saw in chapter 4, determining just how widely we should characterize the functional role of a mental state is very challenging.

Debate over the extent to which the physical realizers of mental states are embodied or extended continues. These proposals have had a dramatic influence on how we think about the mind. Philosophical inquiries into the different kinds of mental state must consider the place that our body and our environment might play in constituting those mental states. And scientific inquiries into the workings of mental processes must consider looking beyond the brain to these wider physical realizers. So even though functionalism gives us a *general* account of how the material brain realizes mental states, these more *specific* questions about the relationship between mind and matter are ripe for discussion and have potentially dramatic implications.

6.2.2 The Knowledge Question

Recent work has also shed new light on the Knowledge Question. Considerable attention has been paid to how we gain knowledge of other minds. One influential proposal developed by philosophers and psychologists in tandem has been that we make judgements about other people's mental states by *simulating* their situation. Philosophers like Jane Heal argue that when we judge what's going on in Mindy's mind, we go through an unconscious mental process of imagining what *we* would be thinking in that situation. If this simulation tells us that *we* would be nervous in her situation, this can feed into the conclusion that *Mindy* feels nervous. This raises interesting questions about how such simulations work and whether such simulations can really secure *knowledge* of other minds.

Recent work on self-knowledge includes valuable research on the knowledge we have of our own conscious experiences. As we have seen in previous chapters, the standard view has always been that we have a very good knowledge of what our own experiences are like. This self-knowledge has a special kind of authority, with some saying that we cannot be wrong about our own conscious experiences. In chapter 5, we even considered the possibility that illusions about conscious experience are impossible. However, recent work has called this standard view into doubt. Eric Schwitzgebel (2006), for example, has drawn on numerous empirical studies –

including his own exercises in 'experimental philosophy' – to argue that the knowledge we have of our own experiences is much more limited than we realize.

As you look at this text, your visual experience has a central region that is very clear and a peripheral region that is less clear. Reading this bit of text, your visual experience is clear enough to discriminate all of the letters, but if it was at 90° from your eyes it would be too blurry to read. So here's the question: how wide is the clear region of your visual experience? Most of us would answer that it's quite wide – maybe around the 30° mark. And it's hard to see how we could be wrong about this. All we have to do is reflect on the visual experience we're currently having and report where it starts to get fuzzy. But multiple considerations suggest we dramatically *overestimate* how wide the clear region of our visual experience is. Psychological research shows that our ability to discriminate colours and shapes starts to drop off dramatically outside just one or two degrees of our visual field, which is roughly equivalent to the width of your thumb when held out at arm's length. This is partly because of anatomical features of the eye and partly because of how resources are distributed in the brain's visual system. The result of all this is plausibly a visual experience that is rich in a very narrow area of the visual field and fuzzy thereafter.

Daniel C. Dennett offers a simple experiment to show how much we overestimate the richness of our experience. Hold out a playing card at arm's length at 90° from your body. Unsurprisingly, you won't be able to recognize what card you're holding. Now, if you gradually bring your arm round to the centre of your field of vision, how far do you think you have to get before you'll be able to discern what the card is? The results will surprise you. We think our visual experience is rich enough to tell us what the card is very quickly, but actually we can get a long way before our visual experience even specifies what colour it is. A huge number of experimental studies provide us with similarly surprising results.

This challenge to our knowledge of consciousness presents serious difficulties for the study of conscious experience. We have seen already that conscious experience is difficult to study *from the outside*. But now it looks like it's also difficult to investigate *from the inside*. If someone reports that their conscious experience feels a certain way, we cannot take their report at face value. The result is that we're left with an aspect of the mind that seems to elude investigation from all angles. This presents a major methodological challenge for philosophers and cognitive scientists alike. Furthermore, it puts a different slant on the illusionist view of phenomenal consciousness discussed in chapter 5. Against illusionism, it is argued that we cannot be mistaken about our conscious experiences. But the foregoing casts serious doubt on this confident stance. And once we have conceded that we can be wrong about our conscious experiences, the possibility of our being wrong that we even have conscious experiences might have to be taken more seriously.

6.2.3 *The Distribution Question*

When it comes to the question of which things have minds and which things don't, there are no easy answers. Historically, the way we've thought about non-human minds has been somewhat anthropocentric. We start with features of the *human* mind, then look to see which beings have those features. A problem with this approach is that it leaves us blind to the possibility of beings with minds dramatically different to our own. The problem goes back at least to Descartes, who thought that animals were mindless automata and that our rational minds – made in the image of God – were the only minds in nature. Today, though, we have a much richer understanding of the different *kinds* of mind that a being might have. We can look through the history of evolution and see how mental capacities developed gradually. We can look at the animal kingdom and see a variegated hierarchy of mental sophistication. And we can look at the development of a human infant and see the incremental formation of a mind.

Debate still continues about where on these continua we should draw the line between the mental and the non-mental. Nevertheless, our grasp of the continua themselves has improved dramatically. We have increasingly sophisticated frameworks for thinking about different levels of perception, reasoning, language, memory, imagination, self-awareness and so on. Furthermore, we have increasingly sophisticated *tests* for determining whether, and to what degree, a being has these mental capacities. For example, the mirror test is a valuable tool for determining whether a creature has a particular level of self-awareness. A red spot is put on the creature's face while they are under anaesthetic then, when they are awake, they are given access to a mirror. If the creature responds to their reflection by touching the spot, then they pass the test, and if they do not, then they fail. The idea is that this reveals whether the creature can recognize a reflection as themselves.

One of the weightiest components of the Distribution Question remains the distribution of *conscious* minds. Illusionism and property dualism remain important parts of the discussion. Some have developed more modest versions of illusionism in which consciousness is real but misconceived. Once we've stripped away these misconceptions, we can start to formulate robust criteria for the possession of consciousness. Property dualists maintain that phenomenal consciousness is non-physical but have sought to establish the physical *correlates* of consciousness. For instance, a scientific theory called information integration theory attempts to offer a mathematical measure of how much consciousness there is in a system. And some property dualists have proposed that physical fields of integrated information are accompanied by non-physical fields of integrated conscious experience. Panpsychism remains a live possibility on such a view but with the added advantage of a positive theory of how little bits of consciousness combine to form complex fields of conscious experience.

6.3 The Future of the Mind

So far we've looked at the leading theories that philosophers of mind have put forward to date. But what kind of theory might they put forward tomorrow? Perhaps it will be a radical new proposal that finally yields a consensus view on the nature of the mental. For what it's worth, I think that such a revolution is unlikely. There just doesn't seem to be room for a theory that departs that much from the existing options. If mental states aren't immaterial states, behavioural patterns, brain states or functional roles, then what are they? And even if a genuinely novel proposal was put forward, I doubt that it could achieve widespread agreement. As we've seen, there are lots of different explanatory targets that a theory of the mental should hit. And since no theory is likely to hit all the targets successfully, there will always be space for a critic to reject it. The more likely course is that subtle refinements will be made to our existing theories and to our conception of the explanatory targets, which shift the balance of opinion a bit without yielding any clear consensus. That said, many revolutionary theories seem inconceivable right up until the day they appear, so we shouldn't dismiss this more dramatic possibility out of hand.

Of course, progress in the philosophy of mind needn't be at the level of an overarching theory of the mental. There are plenty of fine-grained philosophical questions to which exciting new answers will be found. The philosophical questions that gain the most attention will depend on the pressing issues of the time. Implicit bias, for example, is not a topic that is being studied out of mere intellectual curiosity. It's being studied because efforts to make the world more just need to be supported by an understanding of how bias works. So what will be important to us in the coming years? One obvious topic will be AI. As more and more sophisticated artificial minds are created, philosophical questions about artificial minds will become more urgent. Are artificial minds really minds? Can an artificial mind be conscious? Should an artificial being have rights? Furthermore, the emergence of cognitive enhancement technologies will raise challenging questions about the place of artificial enhancements in the human mind. If I start to store my memories on a silicon chip, are they still my memories? Can I use technology to share mental states with others? How might cognitive enhancements alter my conscious experiences?

The trend of increasing interdisciplinarity looks set to continue. With more and more researchers reaping the benefits of softer disciplinary boundaries, it is hard to see how those boundaries could harden in the coming years. Might there come a point where the philosophy of mind gets absorbed into a multifaceted study of the mental, disappearing as a discrete field of study? I think it's unlikely. The study of the mind requires us to *bring together* more abstract, conceptual questions about the mind with more concrete, empirical questions. It should never involve getting rid of the former entirely. So long as there are deep conceptual questions about the nature of the mind – questions that cannot be directly answered by the cognitive sciences – there will be philosophers of mind trying their best to answer them.

Key Concepts

Embodied cognition: a mental process is embodied if the physical process that realizes it includes not just the brain but one's wider body.
Extended cognition: a mental process is extended if the physical process that realizes it includes not just the body but one's wider environment.
Mental representations: another way of describing mental states with intentionality.

References and Further Reading

- Susan L. Hurley (1998), *Consciousness in Action*, Cambridge, MA: Harvard University Press, ch 1. Here Hurley makes an influential case in favour of an embodied view of the vehicles of mental processes.
- Andy Clark and David J. Chalmers (1998), 'The Extended Mind', *Analysis* 58(1): 7–19. Reprinted in David J. Chalmers (ed.) (2021), *Philosophy of Mind: Classical and Contemporary Readings*, 2nd edn, New York: Oxford University Press. This paper offers the intriguing case of Otto and his memory notepad.
- Jane Heal (1998), 'Co-Cognition and Off-line Simulation: Two Ways of Understanding the Simulation Approach', *Mind and Language* 13(4): 477–98. Heal develops the idea that we know about the mental states of others by simulating them.
- Eric Schwitzgebel (2006), 'The Unreliability of Naive Introspection', *Philosophical Review* 117(2): 245–73. Excerpt reprinted in Chalmers, *Philosophy of Mind*, op. cit. This paper offers powerful reasons for doubting the reliability of our judgements about conscious experience.

Index